Art for UBI (manifesto)

Art for UBI (manifesto)

Edited by
Marco Baravalle, Emanuele Braga,
Gabriella Riccio

Graphic Design
bruno, Venezia

Editing
Eleonora De Beni

Translation
Gabriella Riccio from Italian to English
[pp. 6, 20, 56] and from Spanish to
English [p. 144]

Photos
Macao [p. 9]
globalproject.info [p. 10]
Il Campo Innocente [p. 16]
Sabrina Cirillo [p. 17]
Román Lores Riego [pp. 145–46,
148, 151–52, 154–56, 158, 160–63,
165–66]

© 2022 bruno
Images and texts © the Authors

First published by bruno
Dorsoduro 2729
30123 Venezia
ISBN: 978-88-99058-36-4
www.b-r-u-n-o.it

Printed by Grafiche Veneziane,
Venice, in September 2022
for Untitled Snc (bruno)

Art for UBI (manifesto)
is part of *IRI Series*
by Institute of Radical Imagination

The aim of the series is to produce
knowledge in common and around
commoning situated at the intersection
between art, pedagogy and activism
for a transition towards post capitalism

Institute of Radical Imagination
www.instituteofradicalimagination.org

Art for UBI (manifesto)

Edited by
Marco Baravalle, Emanuele Braga, Gabriella Riccio

Art for UBI (manifesto)

6
Introduction
Marco Baravalle, Emanuele Braga, Gabriella Riccio

20
Techno-utopia
The new technology challenge to infrastructure ecosystems
Emanuele Braga

40
Artistic projectariat and the struggle for the Universal Basic Income
Kuba Szreder

56
Smash the patriarchy: social reproduction and the invisibility of essential labor
Ilenia Caleo

70
Questioning UBI through the lens of care
Maddalena Fragnito and Raising Care Assembly

90
A Pluriversal Basic Income
Gabriela Cabaña and Julio Linares

110
Financing the Many Worlds: Pedagogies of (Il)liquidity
Erik Bordeleau

128
Art for UBI (manifesto)

144
One Income, Many Worlds
(Performance script)

Appendix

169
Author's profiles

172
List of platforms, collectives and individual contributors to the Art for UBI (manifesto)

Contents

Introduction

Marco Baravalle, Emanuele Braga, Gabriella Riccio

Art for UBI (manifesto) was born as an international platform of artists and activists who came together in winter 2019–2020 around the topics of income, social justice and economic sustainability. Those were the months of the first lockdowns in China, Italy, Europe and soon all over the world. At that time, the *Institute of Radical Imagination*, as an international coalition active in the field of commoning of artistic practices, launched an online self-training space called the *School of Mutation*. In this open school, various discussions and research lines—iterations—began to arise, involving intellectuals, activists, artists, researchers and scholars of various origins and backgrounds.

Art for UBI is one of those iterations, which soon took the form of a political platform, participated by collectives and individuals from several European and non-European countries. The collectives and the individual participants who joined in the *Art for UBI (manifesto)* had different approaches: some brought precise demands addressed to government policies in their countries, some focused on art sector unions, some focused on self-organization of alternative and autonomous economic spaces based on the refusal of work and mutualism. Among them there were precarious artists, cultural managers and operators with very heterogeneous income.

The collective discussion led to a common proposal: the time has come for a transnational positioning of the art workers world to strongly demand a universal and unconditional income for society as a whole.

Many of the collectives to which we belong, come from years of mobilization and activism on this ground, and we are well aware of the richness of art workers struggles, artistic coalitions, guilds, trade unions and militant art, and has its roots in history for generations.

In the discussions of *Art for UBI (manifesto)* we believe two important dimensions emerged: on the one hand, the point of view of art, of artists as workers, of art as production of content and imagery; on the other hand, the role that art has in the transformation of the labor market, housing, economy and social conflicts.

We have been discussing for years the relationship between art and work, between the value of the artist as an author and the collectives' shared artistic paths, between the processes of financialization of the art work in the big events market or in collecting, and the diverse and numerous practices based on cooperation, care and self-management.

What seems relevant to us is a growing awareness of the role that art and culture play within the financial market and in the transformation of the labor market in general. The artistic community, at times more sensitive—and therefore freer, yet less exposed to capture mechanisms—has constituted a resistance to the dominant social model and to the norm it conveys both in the symbolic production and in the lifestyles, while at the same time being an ongoing laboratory to imagine and invent alternative ways of life and production. Now, more and more it is a common understanding that terms such as art, creativity, innovation have played a decisive role in the transition from the agricultural and industrial, to the so-called post-Fordist economies. Work precariousness has grown hand in hand with the multiplication of professional roles and the propensity for multitasking typical of the creative industries. The symbolic and reputational capital increased by artistic and creative experimentation has played an important role in the financialization of real estate markets in the great global metropolises. Concepts such as city-factory, social factory, bio-capitalism, effectively describe this transition: the production of content and material goods is increasingly disseminated in processes of social cooperation where the assembly line and the interdependence of reproductive forces increasingly coincide in indefinitely with the times of life of the whole society.

After a year of discussion within the *School of Mutation*, the *Art for UBI* platform decided to draw up a programmatic manifesto.

Milan, 2021

The *Art for UBI (manifesto)* opens with declaring that the art world demands a universal and unconditional income for all, refusing to invest in corporatist and identitary logics. Art workers no longer ask for category bonuses, privilege rents, or preferential treatments based on the exceptionality of the artistic work, but are fighting for universal social justice. Basic income is first of all a measure that frees up time, and emancipates the worker from the blackmail of exploitation. As David Graeber said, basic income allows us to say "NO" to shit jobs.

Universal income is no welfare or work-conditioned measure, it breaks the logic of unemployment benefits, it is not a measure for those who are waiting to get a job. It is instead the recognition of the value produced by the social cooperation already in place. It is the recognition of a change of phase: after years and years of precarisation process, working conditions

Venice, 2021

have deeply degraded and wage labor is no longer able to distribute enough wealth and purchasing power. Those are the reasons why we need a new form of distribution of liquidity.

Let's face it: the rulers themselves have realized they have reached a threshold of unsustainability. Yet the way they react is schizophrenic and always based in response to the emergency. That's how the 2008 financial crisis was faced, and it has become even more evident during the recent Sars-Covid19 health crisis. Governments have reacted to the effects of the wage crisis with buffer measures, issuing bonuses and grants, reimbursements and cash-backs, job category by job category. All measures that step by step have tried to avoid social revolt which could have arisen from the explosive economic situation faced with falling wages, higher and higher cost of living, and rampant rising unemployment levels. Thus transforming welfare into a bureaucratic jungle of implemented exceptional micro-measures.

From the art worker's perspective we know too well how much our time is now vampirized by project writing, and heavy bureaucracy, where most of our energies are used to demonstrate again and again that our production is useful to society. Mountains of bureaucracy and a huge waste of time, only to demonstrate what is already evident to everyone: whoever takes care of society and its reproduction produces great value, the most essential value, and for this very reason an income in liquidity must be distributed alongside a universal access to essential services.

Art for UBI (manifesto) is also explicitly linking the history of the refusal of work to the transfeminist, decolonial and ecological perspectives. The manifesto recognizes a fundamental point of inheritance in the history of feminism. In particular of Marxist feminism that has fimrly indicated the exploitation and invisibility of the reproductive workforce as the architrave on which capitalism is based. In this last phase of late capitalism, this balance of power is increasingly evident. Profit is accumulated not only in the exploitation of wage labor, but to a large extent, by not recognizing and invisibilizing care work. Precisely on this lack of recognition of care work that an unconditional universal income must leverage to arm with conceptual legitimacy a post-labor distribution of liquidity.

From the decolonial perspective, the manifesto emphasizes that the precariousness of the labor market is increasingly racializing within the economically stronger states, while the most tiring, poorly paid, and degrading tasks are being outsourced to the global market, concentrating them in those countries that once were their colonies. The universal distribution of income would allow first of all to indistinctly recognize the right to a worthy life for all.

Finally, the ecological perspective. If basic income breaks the chains of degrading work blackmail, it also offers the possibility of breaking blackmail by our present way of production that exploits the planet. UBI answers one of the political questions that has strongly extended through the twentieth century:

Marco Baravalle, Emanuele Braga, Gabriella Riccio

the blackmail between health and work. For a little salary the working class has been constantly forced to get poisoned and to poison the planet. We believe that UBI can inaugurate the process of liberation from this model of progress and production. It allows us to reply to the claim that has dominated the political arena from the 1980s onwards: there is no alternative.

The ecological criticism can open a further perspective to overcome the Capitalocene. Just as universal and unconditional income is based on the recognition of the value produced by human reproductive labor and social cooperation, it is urgent to extend this recognition also to non-human reproduction. The planet as an ecosystem, and the living environment of the biosphere continue to reproduce resources whose fundamental value should be recognized rather than going on relating to them in an extractive way. As much as we want to break the chains of wage exploitation among humans proposing a distribution of wealth as recognition of reproductive alliances and interdependencies, we should also break the chains of the exploitation of the planet's resources labor introducing a culture of interspecies or pluriversal recognition. Listening and recognizing how other agencies—non-human actors—work daily in symbiosis to maintain and reproduce the biosphere.

This allows us to introduce the index of this book, which we thought of in the form of cartography. A political cartography that is able to break the chains of exploitation through a cosmogony that proposes other cardinal points, other reference stars.

In their *Progetto d'un Manifesto* (1941), Altiero Spinelli and Ernesto Rossi, anti-fascists in exile on the Tyrrhenian Island of Ventotene, mention the income of existence as one of the conditions for a free and united Europe.

Human solidarity turned towards those who succumb in the economic battle ought not, therefore, be shown with the same humiliating forms of charity that produce the very same evils it vainly attempts to remedy. Rather it must take a series of measures which unconditionally guarantee a decent standard of living for everyone, without lessening the stimulus to work and to save. In this situation, no one would any longer be forced by misery to accept unfair work contracts.

The clamors and horrors of the Second World War did not succeed in silencing this "confined" voice that would become, in the following decades, a reference point for those who fight against nationalism and against the wars fought in the name of sovereignty and imperialism.

Eighty-one years later, the interventions inspired by our much more modest *Art for UBI (manifesto)* reactivated, albeit in a semi-conscious form, the link between universal income and the critique of national sovereignty.

Gabriela Cabaña and Julio Linares in their essay in this volume articulate against the capitalist apparatus of nation-state and private banks that, beating the drum of war and debt, impose the present model of money and monetary policies. They maintain today more than ever UBI looks to a new internationalist project, in its nature even pluriversal, that is, capable of supporting through policies of commoning and solidarity the right to difference of self-governing communities.

Erik Bordelau argues the importance of unfolding liberation projects not only against finance, but also within and through finance; that is, to update the movements' arsenal with tools capable of pushing the markets towards a liquidity crisis and, at the same time, realizing the potential of a radical cosmos-finance.

Like other contributions in this book, Bordelau's is crossed by a speculative vein not naively utopian, open to fiction, and to the imagination of alternative presents and futures. We like to

Marco Baravalle, Emanuele Braga, Gabriella Riccio

think that the struggle around UBI (therefore also his theory) is a specific genre of that "poetry of the future" Marx hopes for when thinking of the revolution of his time. Not a financial exercise to forecast future scenarios, but one of radical imagination that offers itself, lives, and emerges in the struggles.

An interesting element that emerges from this collection is that, today, UBI grammars seem to be substantiated above all as an assembly of on the one side a radical criticism of the present as nationalist, capitalist and patriarchal; on the other side and imagination/performativity moving in the present towards the future. Turning to the history of art it is possible to identify an antecedent (albeit by no means immediate) of this political-aesthetic linkage. After Ventotene, we may look at another 'island' in times of war: *Cabaret Voltaire* in Zurich, founded in 1916 in the midst of the First World War. T.J. Demos argues that Dadaists geographical displacement in Switzerland is reflected in their poetic techniques of linguistic displacement, which gave rise to what the scholar defines an *heteroglossia*: a different language that had unlearning and abolition of the official language as its premise now unable to articulate itself outside the nationalist rhetoric.

Also today we see how the battle for a multi-universal basic income cannot be separated from the battle against the device of the sovereign nation-state. But Dada is also poetic of fortuity, the breakthrough of the ready-made, the overthrow and mockery of the patriarchal and warmongering accelerationism of (Italian) Futurism. In essence, it is a critique of the political economy of art, and of what today we would call the extractivism of modern capitalism. For example, Maurizio Lazzarato has identified in Duchamp the traits of a pioneering refusal of work, the same refusal that animates the mobilization for UBI with his request to unhook, once and for all, income from the work performance, and even more so in a moment in which capitalism contradiction was made really visible—think of the pandemic—between the centrality of care labor and its lack of recognition by the neoliberal device.

UBI is radical imagination, yet the new worlds towards which it tends, do not derive from any reformist illusions and are not actualized in intentional communities. The micro-utopias, and the community experiments that artists and non-artists carry out, are not the horizon—upon which one comfortably rests with the alibi of capitalist realism. Rather, they are experiments of aesthetic-political subversion of capitalist abstraction, that is, of the general condition of the social relationship. Glimpses of UBI new worlds appear at the heart of prefiguration—another term summoned by the authors of this collection—which takes shape only in broadened social dynamics, in the unexpected, constituent and conflictual spaces opened up by the struggles for the commons.

In this sense, Ilenia Caleo and Kuba Szreder contributions bring us back to the materiality of the struggles and the centrality of the investigation. The terrain, according to Szreder, is that of the organization of the *projectariat*, that's to say that fragmented galaxy of art and cultural workers. The challenge for Szreder, is to move beyond the obsolete belief in the exceptional nature of artistic work, to overcome corporatism, and to promote mutualism and interdependence. Caleo moves from the theoretical perspective of a vital and feminist materialism to affirm that art is not an innocent field. Indeed, it is a space marked by sexist, patriarchal and neocolonial logics. To defeat them, transfeminist struggles must intersect with decolonial and income struggles, overcoming the boundaries of identity politics.

How are mobilizations' achievements supported and substantiated? Emanuele Braga suggests the need to create what the movements define as "institutions of the common." Through

Rome, 2021

his personal involvement at MACAO in Milan across ten years of struggles between financial crisis in 2008 and the health crisis in 2020, Braga constructs a genealogy of the action of social movements at the intersection of digital, creativity and finance, clarifying the terms of a dialectic that contrasts profit-extractivism dichotomy, with care-mutualism linkage.

Raising Care assembly contribution to this collection focuses on the theme of care defined as *"nothing intrinsically 'natural', nor 'nice' or 'maternal', rather it is about the struggles against the current necropolitical management of lives."* Starting from here, the text proceeds with the proposal to combine the struggle for UBI with that for UBS (Universal Basic Services), that is, for essential welfare services such as housing, health care and education. Too often UBI and UBS are presented as alternatives, if not in opposition. Raising Care, on the other hand, invites us to unite them towards UPL, an Unconditional Planetary Livability, i.e. not linked to external evaluations or to the measurement of a performance, capable of keeping together UBI emphasis on self-determination, with the importance UBS puts on care for the social infrastructure, and this within a planetary framework that takes into account the complexity of the web of life on the planet.

We started *Art for UBI* as a radical pedagogy project within the *School of Mutation*. Our self-educating online assembly was transformed into a political platform which led to the drafting of the manifesto. In the following months, in the Spring of 2021, the manifesto was publicly read in several cities by activists—during the Covid-19 pandemic occupations or demonstration actions—claiming art workers rights during the economic crisis. The manifesto appeared in the banners of the temporary occupation of great European theaters such as the Globe in Rome or the Piccolo Teatro in Milan, in ADL Cobas protest squares in Venice, or in the MK&G program in Hamburg. All this was possible because some of the collectives that had joined in the path such as MACAO, Campo Innocente, Sale Docks then reported these claims in their squares, occupations, agendas and local programs.

Naples, 2020

This allows us to introduce how we relate to militant research. To discuss, to invent new concepts, to let them set from a theoretical point of view is never disconnected from the social processes and the transformative tension the paths of struggle have.

Marco Baravalle, Emanuele Braga, Gabriella Riccio

Rather, we consider these plans as connected, the one follows the other, and in the spiral of history they feed at times in a progressive way, sometimes in a non-linear way.

In the history of Italian workerism, the concept of militant research owes its reference to that of *conresearch*, defined by Romano Alquati as the posture with which knowledge is made in the struggle, and in a continuous process of investigation among the oppressed. It is only by questioning the needs and points of view of oppressed subjectivities that research can be done, that a common knowledge can be built and configured. Not an ideology, but a mobile political consciousness that provides theoretical tools for conflict. Furthermore, this type of knowledge-with or situated knowledge of the struggle also has a performative value. It is a practice inserted in a historical tension, in a process of mutation, of transformation of the existing. In short, the concept of conresearch and militant research rejects a division of labor in which the intellectual interprets the historical process and indoctrinates the oppressed on how and why they should fight. Just as it does not propose the opposite: a struggle that does not need knowledge. On the contrary, rebellion is also done through distancing, it is done through the right to intermittence, through the claiming of spaces and times other than the time of work and exploitation. At this junction the *Institute of Radical Imagination* places the production of the work of art. The performance, the exhibition, the show, the image gain meaning within this militant research process. Indeed, militant research could not exist without art and without performance. We refuse to conceive of art as detached from the political process, in a purely ornamental function or as a luxury commodity. Instead, we think creating languages that know how to train, to transform, to affect our individual and collective perception is essential to promote effective paths for the struggles and build common knowledge.

That is why *Art for UBI (manifesto)* turned into a performance. We were looking for an artistic and performative form in which the enquiry carried out in the different territories would translate into the formalization of a staging open to political debate. The spark lit when Anna Rispoli—one of the artists who participated in our platform—told us she was invited to open the Vienna Theater Festival (*Wiener Festwochen*) and she was thinking of doing a performance on UBI. We immediately began to collaborate. Anna organized a survey on the perception of income in Austria. We collaborated under her direction in the drafting of the dramaturgy of the show with the title *Income the Unconditioned Speech*. After a few months, we proposed the same experience of performative research to the community of Madrid, and we staged another performance at the Reina Sofia Museum under the title *One Income, Many Worlds (Una Renta, Muchos Mundos)*. Here we publish the complete dramaturgy of the show staged in Madrid in September 2021.

September 2022

Marco Baravalle, Emanuele Braga, Gabriella Riccio

Techno-utopia
The new technology challenge
to infrastructure ecosystems

Emanuele Braga

What is the link between art, technology and income in the first 20 years of this millennium?

To answer, I provide some coordinates that, in my opinion, have operated within social movements, starting from an analysis of the historical situation and some practices of conflictual and prefigurative self-organization in Italy.

At the beginning of the millennium, we artists realized we were at the center of the wider transformation of the job market.

Boltanski and Chiapello in *The New Spirit of Capitalism* pointed out how creativity as a concept was at the core of traditional labor market dismantlement, and at the same time it was the model around which the new forms of precarious labor market were being built. In those same years, Paolo Virno in *A Grammar of the Multitude* drafted an anthropological portrait of precariousness describing the political implications of the creative condition of the entrepreneur of the self, with its performativity and temporality based on the event.

Some new categories came up such as the multitasking way of working, the dismantling of the rigid grid of the division of labor as regulated by the various guilds and professional associations, the exaltation of the figure of the entrepreneur of the self, the role of reputation, the economy of attention, contracts deregulation, the figure of the freelance. They have all glorified the flexible and competitive model based on the ability to innovate and be creative.

On closer inspection, this process developed in parallel with the appearance of the digital economy on a global scale. The productive model of the web economy (Web 1) up to the platform economy (Web 2) inserted in this passage between Fordism and post-Fordism, at the same time of the glorification of creativity as the incentive for building-up precariousness.

New technologies and creativity are two of the pillars of the precarious work paradigm shift.

The birth of the Internet put concepts like collaboration and sharing at the center. Yet soon the open-source idea—where accessibility and collaboration prevail over copyright and ownership—turned into an opportunity for capital to privatize, at low cost, social cooperation. Then we get to the sharing economy and the consumer/producer models—where starvation wages prevail: one is pushed to work nonstop, also for free, and at the advantage of large proprietary platforms that make a profit out of it and, as never before, manage to act as monopolies.

The third pillar of job transformation is finance. In a progression that is more and more out of control, finance becomes a value-accumulation protagonist. The consequence was the emergence of debt as a new tool for controlling public policies and welfare cuts. At the same time, though, it was an anthropological tool in the construction of the subjectivity of each individual. Maurizio Lazzarato accompanies this passage describing the anthropological characteristics of the figure of the indebted man. Through debt it is possible to control the slow productivity of an infinite number of subjects and collectives, no matter what they produce. On the other hand, finance, through the construction of derivatives, becomes more and more distant from the real economy, and increasingly able to condition and control commodity markets as well as state public policies. In macroeconomics the emerging paradigm is: wage labor and employment under any contractual form are no longer able to be the main vectors of income distribution. In short, by setting ourselves free from the assembly line, we thought we could use time to build a world tailored to our rights and desires, starting from the sharing of our knowledge and means of production. Instead, we found ourselves in a more competitive world, where we work at low intensity, perpetually under the blackmail of debt, and where everything costs more and more, the price of raw materials and technologies being in the hands of very few private monopolies. According to economists, the progression that lead us to this situation was: first, we see a sharp wage drop; second, this deflationary thrust coexists with a growing monopolistic power in the sectors indicated above; third, the combination of these two phenomena reduces purchasing power; and finally the result is that through economic crises, the super rich get richer and richer, jobs get increasingly scarce and shitty, and prices skyrocket.

Automation and the birth of the web instead of freeing up time and providing the opportunity for the invention of more emancipated forms of life based on cooperation and sharing, generated—on global scale—an acceleration of the production and extraction of raw materials, and an overall impoverishment of society, with more and more precarious work and less and less access to welfare services.

For this reason, talking about techno-utopia gets more and more difficult. After all, technology seems not such a great ally to social and climate justice.

But in the folds of these three pillars—creativity, finance and the digital—social movements started conceiving an alternative use of technologies. In fact creativity, finance and the digital are the three most interesting territories in which we have been trying to act in conflict and social struggle.

From the 1990s through the 2010s, talking about techno-politics really meant believing one could redesign society. The Internet was born out of the will of some academic research centers, with the aim to work in real time on contents shared by different peers or nodes. Those were the years in which the digital was such a new territory as to feed the feeling that the new self-managed digital infrastructures could be autonomous and counter-hegemonic. Projects such as *Indymedia, Hackmeetings, the Free Software Movement*, really aspired to a generational revenge, inventing new production models that could avoid capture by capital and thus scale up in a distributed way, eventually replacing the big and old industrial monopolies.

In those years the digital met the creative, most of the time inside people's garages where they weren't paying any rent. But venture capitalism transformed them into Silicon Valley and platform capitalism. Social networks born as platforms for sharing and producing media and information content soon turned into digital platforms for housing, transport, goods logistics and finance.

The great extractive maneuver blocking the emancipatory power expressed by techno-political counter-hegemonic projects lies in this very passage to Web 2, which is the first infrastructure for enhancing personal information and conditioning user behavior at the origin of a real anthropological transformation aimed at governing anti-capitalist cooperative dynamics.

Towards the end of the first decade, during the initial hype of Web 2, the financial crisis broke out. The New Economy needed financial markets to obtain the resources necessary to support innovative and largely intangible projects to measure the value of what was at that time unmeasurable. It is evident how this process led to speculation. Innovative dynamics facilitated access to credit over time, and the logic of easy credit affected the subprime sector. Finance turned out to be a huge speculative bubble more and more disconnected from the real economy, whose only purpose was to get half the world into the trap of debt.

What did social movements do during this collapse of finance? They occupied squares, streets and spaces of public discussion. They did so camping in public spaces, forming circles in which to pass the microphone from hand to hand to decide together. This happened in NY as well as in Milan, Madrid, Barcelona, Cairo, London and Istanbul.

Many focused on this one detail: the form of organization of struggles against finance are the assembly circles in Zuccotti Park, Tahrir Square, Gizi Park, those of the Indignados, or of the Italian occupied theaters; the tents, the mics passed around in assemblies, the media center, the method of consensus, the division into working groups, the deliberative process, the raised hands, the signs to ask to speak and ask questions... Social movements respond to finance with a new aesthetic of being together to share one's precarious condition and decide together what's to be done. They respond with this new code of conduct, with an "assembly" technique. The way in which struggles are organized is in and of itself an alternative social technology. A new procedure existing institutions have to deal with.

While digital platform algorithms progressively control society through datification and behavior automation, the social body responds with its dissident algorithms, most of the time with analog algorithms, rules of being together, and occupying the public space showing their need and authoritativeness to organize in a different way. The social body wants to reprogram from the bottom up. It knows how to self-determine its own codes of conduct and organizational forms. When the capital starts programming society through the digital, the social body responds with alternative forms of self-organization, showing its intention to program alternative life algorithms.

The concept of techno-politics extends from the programming of alternative and independent media and their conflictual use, to the tactical use of media, the programming of organizations, relational forms, independent and conflictual decision-making processes.

If through datification and algorithmic control capital is able to value and shape social behaviors, the social body increasingly acquires awareness of being willing to self-determine the use of platforms, data and programming.

After the financial crisis and the occupy movement, between the 2010s and 20s in Europe, the time had come for this reflection. Are we able to create independent technological infrastructures? How much has it to do with the digital, and how much has it also to do with techniques of self-organization as social beings? Is coding an anonymous wallet and a good algorithm enough? Or should we also institute new forms of political organization? Programming code strips must go hand in hand with programming militant forms of organization.

What I want to emphasize is that the movement's response to the financial crisis generated a new level of consistency. The stakes changed. We moved from the centrality of unionization, denouncing privatizations and cuts in public spending (no-global struggles against WTO), to the search for alternative forms of organization of common action. We called it the "constituent" or "instituting" dimension of the struggles.

This change of plan within the movements generated also a relevant change in the art system and its aesthetic paradigms.

Many individual or collective artists and curators began creating real fiction projects in which the medium is the instituting form or the organizational form itself. Artists, instead of only using mediums like video, music, sculpture or canvas, started to create relational rituals: saunas, pizza ovens, museums, fake nation states, secret services, 2.0 trade unions, offshore companies in tax havens, algorithms capable of attacking financial markets, agricultural cooperatives, wet labs, banks and universities.

It is no longer a matter of inventing objects or shapes on a sheet of paper, but of creating social architectures, rituals and organizational forms. And more important, it is no longer a question of working only on the symbolic, but also practicing those forms in the first person, in everyday life, in one's own biography, bending the concept of the performative in the field of the representation, to the field of the political and social power relations. It is certainly not a question of killing the symbolic—fiction and representation—but rather of passing *from* the level of the symbolic, *to* that of the real power relations, from aesthetics to conflict, in an organic, schizophrenic, destabilizing way, acquiring more and more awareness of the process of mutation, transformation, queerization that these steps trigger in one's body. In some cases this gray area muddied the waters to the point that the arising question was whether the artist had turned into a manager, a social worker, an activist, a farmer, a chemist or a financial speculator.

Getting back to the red thread of Techno-utopia. If the question of the control and automation of our social behaviors was among the most increasingly felt political problems this millennium has brought up, I believe the aesthetic and conflicting political response can be traced back to our desire for autonomy and re-appropriation of one's ability to program, to determine one's own bodies, to conceive of organizations, to manage and to assemble.

MACAO, an independent art center in Milan I have been a member of, was initiated in 2012 as part of the Italian art workers movement in response to the financial crisis. MACAO has been a workshop experimenting on forms of being together, sharing means of production, and the centrality of care at the expense of competition.

As with many other artists movements, one of the most important research fields of those years was precisely the concept of economics. Partly for a very practical reason: we were all penniless, forced to accept shitty jobs, always anxious to constantly promote ourselves in that very selective and increasingly precarious market. Mutualism was our response. Yet we asked ourselves the question lying at the root of the problem: what do we value? Do we value professional competition, a glittering screen object, an exclusive service? All those being not just very expensive, but also obscure objects of desire. Why do we value them so much? Why do we respect a man in a suit and tie coming out of a skyscraper in a bit of a hurry, more than a guy who looks at the ceiling sprawled out on a dirty sofa? Why are the derivatives that the man in a suit and tie just sold worth more than the thoughts of the boy sprawled out on the dirty sofa?

We never were fans of degrowth, but we have always felt the need to question the current productive and reproductive system. The question around what we truly value is to be constantly put at the center.

In those same years another very disruptive phenomenon emerged: the Bitcoin. A community of hackers across the globe developing a protocol to securely transact value units without a centralized infrastructure framework. A new technological innovation was quietly worming its way into the scene. It showed up as all true technical innovation: a gesture of rupture launched by some anarchic activists against the central banking system, for the first time capable of making finance shake.

For sure, it was the assembly of something new: cryptography made it possible to create a secure object one could trust, not because it was guaranteed by a government or an institution, but instead by a globally distributed network of peers.

Bam! Perfect, ten years later today we know this breaking gesture also aspired to update the Internet to a new geological era, making it jump from Web 2 to Web 3, from the social networks internet to the distributed data internet.

In 2013 we came up with the idea to host for a month at MACAO in Milan an international Bitcoin community camp. As in a commune, we lived together and talked a lot. At the end of the month, we also organized a meeting between the (now) very famous first developers of Bitcoin and Etherum and Richard Stallman, Free Software Foundation founder.

The following year, though—among several italian theorists, artists and activists—we talked a lot about that meeting, and decided to call a summit within the community linked to post-workerism and the history of Italian autonomy, which we titled *La moneta del Comune (The Currency of the Common)*.

We were wondering if Bitcoin really was the Currency of the Common, that counter-systemic and revolutionary currency. And our answer was no, it wasn't.

The problem with cryptocurrencies is that they did not undermine the competitive, individualistic and proprietary system inscribed in the traditional financial system. In the architecture or design of a technology, one can inscribe a large part of the social body that it will generate... It is no different from biology or constitutional models. Every technology is always also a cosmotechnique, a way of worldmaking.

Circulation scarcity and therefore value volatility, as well as speculative object flexibility are all inscribed in the Bitcoin algorithm. It is inscribed that it is going to be energetically very wasteful, as well as safe, reliable, anonymous and transparent. The power of Bitcoin is the style in which its architecture is written, which is so minimal. In very few steps Bitcoin could generate a distributed, non-centralized, anonymous and secure infrastructure. Yet soon it was mostly used by the very same system it was trying to destroy. Indeed it became the new speculative finance *enfant prodige*, handled by centralized brokerage platforms, whose apps landed on the mobile phones held by greedy hands of millions of go-getting white boys.

In short, we wondered: what is the use of a cryptocurrency if it only excites the speculative mechanism of western individualistic proprietary competition at crazy energy costs? We understood blockchain architecture itself was not enough to make a difference from a political point of view. Technological innovation should go hand in hand with institutional innovation. If technologies change while institutions do not, the result stays the same.

Instituting a new way of being together though, would require working on political and cultural assumptions rather than just on technology. Technology can be bent and developed in one direction or another according to the political tension in which it settles. We can determine the complex system of which we are technically composed only on condition that we are in a conscious process of mutation and transition.

Between 2014 and 2019 at MACAO the new challenge was: how through crypto wallets, alternative currencies, organizational systems capable of affecting economic space, income and the division of labor, to politically daunting competition, debt, scarcity and piecework, while at the same time promoting forms of behavior based on cooperation, sharing, mutual help, the gift economy, and freeing up time instead of wasting it?

So we started developing alternative economic spaces in which to experiment in this direction, programming our own tools, and above all trying to understand what organizational forms and social rituals we needed.

Specifically, at MACAO in collaboration with *dyne.org*, Jaromil Denis Roio and the *D-cent* project, we developed the *Common Coin* social portfolio. For years, the MACAO assembly discussed how to distribute money—whose liquidity was not scarce—since it was generated by ourselves in a way that could encourage mutualism between projects, enhance collaboration, and at the same time recognize the value of the enormous amount of regularly invisible work. We tried to reject any centralized evaluation scheme based on ranking systems and revenue models. Instead, as much as possible we tried to link the attribution of value to self-evaluation and community discussion. What we value has always remained an open question and is always the driving force of disputes, discussions and narratives. Value, rather than being a unit of accounting, is an archive of never truly quantifiable narratives, a mobile field of tensions of subjects in relation to each other. We decided that tokens (*Common Coin*) would condition and give access to common wallets in euros. Based on the circulation of *Common Coin*, the community of MACAO decided to regulate the distribution of common wallets of the value produced by the organization in euros.

In those same years, Ethereum (2016) launched, with a few flops, the DAO, Decentralized Autonomous Organization. What prominently stands out is that crypto coins are leaving the stage to a new protagonist: the blockchain. This distributed way of data storage in a single blockchain underlying cryptocurrencies was launched as the new diva. Through blockchain is it possible not only to make coins, but also to infrastructure social and corporate bonds, to vote and to stipulate contracts.

We were not too much interested in the development of Ethereum and DAOs from a technical and operational point of view, yet we recognized a similarity with what was happening with *Common Coin* at MACAO: more than a currency, these tokens can define the social and corporate bonds within an organization.

During those years we started collaborating with the *Faircoin* project. Faircoin was founded by a group of people including Enric Duran. Enric had stolen several hundred thousand euros from Spanish banks to finance social centers and alternative finance projects, and since then has been declared an international fugitive. That group founded the global Faircoop cooperative made up of independent agricultural producers, freelancers, distributors and activists who decided to use a cryptocurrency called Faircoin as the main exchange currency. Peculiar to Faircoin: it fixes its value through the Faircoop shareholders' meeting (which takes place on Telegram) and at the same time also leaves a certain amount of Faircoin on the financial markets to arbitrage, where value is decided by crypto markets.

We set up a Faircoop node at MACAO in Milan, and began to buy food products in Faircoin with collective purchases available at MACAO in *Common Coin*.

After a few years, together with Faircoop, we founded a financial platform where we could manage multi-currency wallets which we called *Bank of the Commons*. In other words, we thought we could provide all members with portfolios in euros, bitcoin, ethereum and faircoins, jointly self-managing an online digital bank.

Ten years later all those experiments failed. Their failure was due to the metamorphosis of the communities, to the underestimation of some tactical choices, to the exogenous prevalence of speculation over the endogenous thrust of cooperation. Nonetheless, for a few years they did work. Then they came to an end, shed their skin, and turned into something else.

Common to these radical experiments in alternative economic spaces, practiced and promoted mostly by anti-capitalist activists, is the need to conceive organizational schemes based on mutualism, solidarity, and on less scarce and more abundant liquidity. In *Bank of the Commons* I had the privilege of meeting and working together with Heloisa Primavera, a well-known Argentine alternative monetary systems activist during the South America economic crisis. The idea and the attempt was to move cryptocurrencies away from anarcho-capitalist ideology and bring them closer to the history of solidarity and circular economy. Two big titans were fighting in the forums and activists' assemblies: communism and anarchy. Personally I have never cheered for either one: on one side the need for individual autonomy, freedom, anonymity, rejection of bureaucracy, on the other side the need to decide together, empower teams of developers and managers, centralize power, levy taxes, and build common actions.

Basic Income was the project that inherited these reflections at MACAO. Somehow ideas born out of the experience with *Common Coin and Bank of the Commons* led our community to develop and increasingly invest in this project for unconditional income distribution in euros to all participants. The largest joint portfolio of MACAO's organization was intended for Basic Income, and fed each week a portion of the budget of each project contributing to MACAO's public program. MACAO's members agreed not to be paid for the development of internal projects, and to wait until the end of the month for the equal distribution of an unconditional income to everybody. Thus we became an art center that does not pay anyone on the basis of work done, but rather distributes an unconditional and equal income to everyone.

Shortly after, in the same year, a community of artists in Brussels, part of our network, shared their desire to start a project called *Common Wallet*: a community of about ten artists, with very different income bases, decides to collectivize income in a single bank account, and gives each member the freedom to withdraw money according to his/her own needs. The only condition is to talk to each other on a weekly basis and discuss in a fixed presential meeting. In Milan this took place during assemblies, in Brussels they gathered around a common breakfast in someone's apartment. But the technology and the ritual are very similar.

We also worked with small and large art institutions interested in experimenting with cryptocurrencies and economic spaces. We tried with Documenta 14 at the invitation of Paul Preciado: the path was at the same time very interesting, difficult and unsuccessful. With a similar idea we had a much better experience in the performing arts in Italy between 2016–2018 with the Santarcangelo Festival: how to create common portfolios to direct the liquidity of these institutions to those who are usually exploited and underpaid? How to create an economic space in which the production of value is a collective, indivisible gesture, in which value can be distributed only with the attitude of taking care of the collective and the ecosystem in which one is immersed?

After these experiments with cryptofinance, digital currencies and with conflicting mutualism in autonomous organizations, it is evident how the concept of Unconditional Basic Income becomes increasingly central even in small-scale experimentations. To improve the quality of one's life, to be able to say no to shitty jobs, to be able to take care of those close to you, to be able to get out of non-stop performance anxiety, the economic field generated by free access to a basic income is considerably productive of ways of worldmaking.

When looking for what technology is needed to build the utopia of a just society, one definitely must put Basic Income in the toolbox. Techno-utopia takes us to the territories of common portfolios, unconditional income, pooling of means of production, and free access to knowledge and resources. Our task is to create interdependence and alliances between those who are developing digital and non-digital tools and are capable of this vision.

These prefigurative experiences—mostly born from the free initiative of bottom-up artists and activists trying to use both technology and the very form of their organization to respond to precarity—have expressed forms of universal distribution of unconditional income.

Following Negri and Hardt, we must find the way in which these forms of prefigurative antagonism can generate new institutions. In the case of Bitcoin, the occupy movement, the self-management activist community assemblies, what we see are precisely gestures of rupture not directly resorbable to the technical organization of capital. Yet they are technically radical enough to be able to question the real. Just like the self-organization of struggles, these prefigurative forms indicate the way to become institutions.

Nonetheless, we must avoid giving in to the temptation of technology fetishism. Bitcoin started as an anti-system gesture, against the banking system and in support of WikiLeaks autonomy. Yet soon financial markets used it as a new speculative tool. In exactly the same way, NFT, whose aim was to emancipate artists from contemporary art market intermediaries, soon was used by Sotheby's or Christie's to beat the auction at unbeatable prices, gradually becoming completely useless, and basically inaccessible with a fee of $100 on each trade. Just like Bitcoin, NFT is now very popular: it can generate a false scarcity, it is but a sign without content, whose value skyrockets just because it is an exclusive and potentially speculative object.

Transforming these prefigurative innovations into new political institutions means questioning central bank governance, each of the nation-state public policies, and the world of private enterprise. Ask them what it means to introduce direct distribution of basic income and a direct injection of liquidity to manage the redistribution of social wealth.

That's the reason why economists such as C. Marazzi, A. Fumagalli, S. Lucarelli and C. Vercellone affirmed the need to act on a "quantitative easing for the people" from the

European Central Bank, digital tax platforms, and financial markets. At the same time they articulate the need for a universal and unconditional income at the national level, which should go beyond any conditionality to access work.

This is the way to become an institution of antagonism to the financial crisis.

In the course of the *Art for UBI (manifesto)* it was evident that a large number of European artists' collectives indicate universal and unconditional income as the necessary economic measure for social justice. As many have pointed out, its move implies an underlying strategic choice. As pointed out at the beginning of this paper, artists are well aware they are at the center of the model of precarization of the entire labor market. For this very reason they demand the distribution of basic income not only for the art world, but for all categories of workers.

Personally I am convinced that the paradigm shift from the centrality of work to the centrality of income and welfare is a conjuncture that both capitalism and the antagonistic forces are coming to face. Since time immemorial the history of feminism explained to us the centrality of care—and not of production!—as a territory of struggle and expropriation of value. The feminist perspective has always focused on this connection. Capital, much faster and with better profit than the exploitation of wage labor, is founded on the invisibilization and exploitation of reproduction. Precisely on this point the circle closes: capital shows in a more and more explicit way that, after all, goods and factories are secondary to natural resources, biotechnology, and the control of behaviors and bodies. Pharmaceuticals, education, information, and energy are the strategic fields of bio-capitalism.

I firmly believe the issue we should increasingly observe, address and condition does not lie in the opposition between

Techno-utopia
The new technology challenge
to infrastructure ecosystems

income and work, but in the different models of income distribution and welfare services.

I believe that states that do not agree to invest at all in basic income and universal services (education, health and freedom of movement) are choosing for war. War, too, is an economic technology not to be underestimated. It could be deliberately undertaken to restore social and geopolitical power relations. Internal war translates into an employment crisis, inflation, and the elimination of welfare. As Saskia Sassen's analysis suggests, war could lead to the *slumization* of European metropolises, creating within Europe itself an apartheid of income and services.

In my opinion, a more likely scenario could be that in which European governance uses income, education, health and transport as tools of social control. The intersection between technological capacities for real-time control of our behaviors and the will of the rulers to condition them through evaluation systems, could put the issue of income and welfare at the center of politics, yet in a top-down moralizing and meritocratic role. Biopolitics could land on government agendas in the form of income policies and investments in welfare and the environment. Capital is shifting its focus from production to reproduction. Therefore, one may think that the progressive policies Europe is embarking on, such as Next Gen EU and the Green New Deal, will develop in the tension between, on the one hand the danger of inflation and employment collapse, and on the other hand in investments in welfare, income, and energy infrastructure conditioned by a huge bureaucratic apparatus of bio-control. For this very reason we fight for the unconditionality and universality of basic income. What is at stake here is to lay the foundation of a positive biopolitics capable of recognizing gift and social cooperation already in place, and to counterattack the idea of biopolitics based on interest groups control in favor of the already clearly addressed planning. In this sense, I believe that the debate on UBI includes the stakes of failure of the modern and colonial relationship with the ecosystem of the biosphere that humans had during the era of Capitalocene. Do we still think we have to ground our cosmotechnique on mass control in order to better shape our domain on resources and society? Or rather should we confederate the living forces that self-determine life cycles of human and non-human reproduction? UBI (Universal Basic Income) and UBS (Universal Basic Services) are the beginning of this journey. A path that puts all subjects, human and non-human, in the condition of being able to choose how to best reproduce our lives. A path that leaves in the background the issue of control and security, and that finally is capable of focusing on listening to the several possible assemblages that vital forces generate. Focusing on defense and affirmation of these virtuous interdependencies. A utopian technology that does not close and does not limit, instead that builds and structures on the basis of the interdependence and the desires of subjects who, up until now, have precarious lives and are oppressed.

Bibliography

Baravalle, Marco. *L'autunno caldo del curatore. Arte, neoliberismo, pandemia.* Venice: Marsilio, 2021.

Braga, Emanuele, and Andrea Fumagalli. *La moneta del comune. La sfida dell'istituzione finanziaria del comune.* Rome: DeriveApprodi, 2015.

Caleo, Ilenia. *Performance, materia, affetti. Una cartografia femminista.* Rome: Bulzoni, 2021.

Boltanski, Luc, and Eve Chiapello. *Le nouvel esprit du capitalisme.* Paris: Gallimard, 1999.

Fragnito, Maddalena, and Miriam Tola. *Ecologie della cura. Prospettive transfemministe.* Rome: Orthotes, 2022.

Fumagalli, Andrea, and Cristina Morini. *Reddito di base. Liberare il XXI secolo.* Milan: Momo Edizioni, 2021.

Lavoratori dell'arte. "Manifesto dei lavoratori dell'arte." Facebook, 2011.

Lazzarato, Maurizio. *La fabbrica dell'uomo indebitato. Saggio sulla condizione neoliberista.* Rome: DeriveApprodi, 2011.

Lovink, Geert, and Ned Rossiter. *Organization after Social Media.* Amsterdam: Minor Compositions, 2018.

Hardt, Michael, and Antonio Negri. *Assembly.* Oxford: Oxford University Press, 2017.

Virno, Paolo. *Grammatica della moltitudine. Per un'analisi delle forme di vita contemporanee.* Catanzaro: Rubattino, 2001.

Terranova, Tiziana. *After the Internet: Digital Networks between Capital and the Common.* Boston: Semiotext(e), 2001.

Artistic projectariat and the struggle for the Universal Basic Income

Kuba Szreder

The Universal Basic Income (UBI) haunts artistic circulation. It calls to artistic projectariat as a spectre of grand transformation that would free them from a relentless grind of freelancing, where in order to stay afloat they have to make one project after another and multiple in the same time.

When in September 2021 I was invited by the Institute for Radical Imagination to discuss the universal basic income at its summit in Madrid, I was tasked with tackling a fundamental question: what are the possibilities to turn (self) exploitation and precarization into mutualism and interdependence among cultural workers, and what role could the UBI play? I quote it at length, as the same question informs this text, which is based on the notes I made in Madrid, and follows up with some of the debates we had there. When I reflected upon this set of problems, I quickly fathomed that we have discussed UBI with clusters of radical art workers for two decades or so. For example, back in 2009, responding to an introduction of the neoliberal cultural policies in Poland, the team of Free/Slow University of Warsaw published the *Manifesto for the Radical Change in Culture*, where we advocated for the UBI as a solution for freelancers working in the arts (Committee for the Radical Change in Culture 2009). It is important to mention that we were criticized for artistic exceptionalism by our comrades affiliated with campaigns for UBI. As they argued, and I wholeheartedly agree with them, UBI in order to achieve what it is designed to do, cannot be devoted to one group only (more on this later). This mistake the IRI's manifesto *Art for UBI* has not only avoided, but forcefully expressed a direct support for the UBI as an equalitarian and universal policy. Even though radical art workers in Poland were hardly pioneers in this field, as the entire debate had started much earlier, they were still one of the early adopters of the idea, at least in this country. As if the notion of the universal basic income fitted very well not only with their ideological tendency, but even more importantly with their class composition, i.e. the patterns structuring how they work, live, and imagine themselves. I developed this basic intuition in the practice-driven inquiries into the work and life of artistic projectariat, the results of which have been recently published as the *ABC of projectariat. Living and working in a precarious art world* (2021). I mention this collective research here, as it grounds the following discussion, in which I will introduce the notion of projectariat and scrutinize its class composition to discuss the allure of the UBI. This analysis will be concluded by analyzing not only what would UBI do for art workers, but rather what would a struggle for UBI entail for their own class consciousness and forms of political organization.

Who is the artistic projectariat?
Before embarking on these debates, a couple of words of introduction are in place, regarding the concept of the projectariat. First of all, this particular wording is a result of linguistic ingenuity of Szymon Żydek, a comrade from the Free/Slow University of Warsaw, who came up with this term when we talked about freelancers working in contemporary art. Back then I used a much more clunky term: project-makers, to emphasize the dominant role that projects play in structuring the apparatuses of cultural production in contemporary art. But projectariat is a much more apt term, as it linguistically and politically harks back to its older comrades-in-arms, i.e. proletariat and precariat. The first one does not require any primer, the latter was introduced recently to discuss the precarisation of labor force forced by neoliberal labor markets (Standing 2014), and has already been criticized from feminist positions for essentialisation of the fundamental condition of precariousness (Lorey 2015).

Setting these debates aside, the projectariat is a slightly cheeky, and yet theoretically sound and practically useful notion. It covers all those freelancers working in contemporary art and cultural industries, such as independent curators, artists, critics, academics, designers, lecturers, producers, fashionistas, educators, NFT minters. All of them work on projects or in other forms of temporary employment, and roam the circuits of contemporary art in search of new assignments. Typically, they have to make projects in order to make a living. To stay in the circulation they have to follow the flow of interchangeable opportunities, always at a threat of exclusion. They are natives of the project-based world, the origins of which were dissected by Luc Boltanski and Eve Chiapello in their seminal work on the *New Spirit of Capitalism* (Boltanski and Chiapello 2005), and more generally discussed in the context of immaterial labor and creative industries (Kunst 2015; McRobbie 2015; Lazzarato 2011; Raunig 2013).

The members of artistic projectariat are typically well-educated professionals, enjoying some of the privileges of North-Western middle-classes, attracted by the promises of creative mobility and youthful enthusiasm, and yet living under a constant pressure of precarity, poverty, exclusion, and depression (diagnosed by Bifo Berardi as professional illness of creative industries [Berardi 2009]). Their professional existence, following Paulo Virno's insightful comments on the neoliberal labor markets and service industry (Virno 2004), is underpinned by opportunism, cynicism, and fear. They are constantly looking for new opportunities, roaming the globe in search of projects or other temporary assignments. Typically, they are ultra-mobile and their professional trajectories push them beyond their local communities (networks connect), thus a temptation for cynical networking, an acquisitive and ultra-competitive mode of free-riding (for this reason Pascal

Gielen criticizes independent curators as global joy riders, loyal to anyone but their own precious portfolios [Gielen 2009]). They live in constant fear of economic and social degradation, which motivates their hectic undertakings (De Carolis 1996).

Regarding the class composition of projectariat, some of the more privileged projectarians share similar traits with a cohort described by Guy Standing as proficiens, i.e. well skilled professionals, who take advantage of the flexible labor market (Standing 2014). Proficiens can do so only because they occupy a thinning *strata* of well paid jobs in law, medicine, finance, science, media, and IT. The vast majority of artistic projectarians, due to the specificity of artistic circulation, with its relatively minor budgets and winner-takes-all economy that skews income curves (0,1% of artists earning millions while thousand are pushed below poverty line [Abbing 2002]), do not enjoy this level of privilege. In this regard, they are much closer to precariat, in constant fear of survival, and thus they are also more eager to become the traitors of their own middle-class origins, to paraphrase Walter Benjamin who quoted Louis Aragon in his discussion on authors as producers (Benjamin 1970). I would argue that this partially explains their willingness to adopt and advocate for such ideas as Universal Basic Income, that—alongside the demand for commons-based infrastructure— would need to fundamentally impair the cycles of capital accumulation, from which wealthier professionals, including 1% of artistic projectarians, benefit (mainly via stocks and properties). Just to press a point that I have implicitly suggested (I discuss this argument more thoroughly in the *ABC of projectariat*): people dwelling is artistic circulation are not a unified formation, but are internally structured following the divisive line of (mostly inherited) privilege, based on class, gender, race and citizenry, that results in extreme inequalities in distribution of economic, cultural, and social capital. There is artistic projectariat, manning networked production lines of artistic factories, there is artistic 1%, who is, as Andrea Fraser would argue, directly aligned with financial oligarchies, a wealthy class of collectors, corporate leaders, speculators, media moguls, and ultra-wealthy art celebrities (Fraser 2011). Their interests do not align, in fact there is a silent class war that artistic projectarians are losing with every billion poured into the art market.

99% of artistic projectarians find their trajectories fragile and jobs temporary. Even people working in institutions are typically stripped of job security. All but the most privileged castes of higher management are exposed to competition caused by systems of academic and artistic evaluation, driven by neoliberal management, and amplified by financial austerity, and/or by political pressures (in countries such as Hungary or Poland). Moreover, most of the institutional operations are structured as if they were projects, triggering an endless repetition of short-term assignments, unpaid internships and precarious zero-hours contracts, with institutions benefiting from structural artsploitation (Kopel 2021). Thus, in spite of having a job and enjoying a semblance of stability, even people working in institutions end up in the same vicious cycle as freelancers, who have to always make one project after another and many at the same time. Systematically coerced to become the entrepreneurs of themselves (Foucault 2011), they have to take individual risks and invest in chasing the flow of passing opportunities, spending enormous amounts of unpaid time just to write applications, follow deadlines, secure resources, administer projects, and write reports. This is the vicious cycle of the projectariat, shared with other segments of precarious workforce: one needs to make a lot of effort, in order to secure paid work (Ross 2009).

The current pandemic has only made it harder. With millions of jobs lost in the creative industries (Sherwood 2022), events suspended, institutions locked, residencies and projects on hold, it has become much harder to find opportunities and make the ends meet in contemporary art (Baravalle 2020; Judah 2020; Steinhauer 2020). For the vast majority of projectarians, the pandemic did not mean a stopover of activities, but rather their frantic acceleration aimed at securing dwindling opportunities. Even public funding that was made available for art workers during the pandemic (a flagship example being an unconditional support received by art workers in Berlin, who at the beginning of pandemic received a free check from government equalling to €5,000 [Artdex 2020]) could not replace the missing incomes. However, the pandemic pressed home an idea that the unconditional basic income can be a viable solution to the maladies of precarity, both in the artistic sector and in a society at large (with schemes such as furlough payments, tax waivers and other direct financial support systems implemented on a mass scale in the global North-West). It is very possible that this interest will be short-lived, thwarted by the rising inflation, debt loop, looming austerity, and yet another wave of neoliberal privatization. But this is a window of opportunity that—even if narrow—recalibrates public perception of the conditions of labor in the distributed factories of contemporary art.

UBI or squaring the vicious cycle of projectariat
And here comes my first hypothesis: the amount of unpaid labor conducted in order to get any job whatsoever is one of the reasons why art workers intuitively support the universal basic income, as it helps them to—at least on a level of political imagination—square the vicious cycle of project-based labor.

This analysis is concurrent with the discussions on precarious labor and the new spirit of capitalism. Guy Standing, for instance, advocates for universal basic income as a remedy for precarity (Standing 2014; 2017). Precarity is particularly detrimental for the people from lower classes, whose lack of financial security paired with structurally limited access to social networks and education, locks them in an endless loop of temporary, unsecure, poorly paid, exploitative and unrewarding jobs. For the precariat the UBI would not only provide a tremendous uplift in their existential prospects, but would also serve as an act of historical justice. The precarity of workers is one of the factors that enables their exploitation, just as in classical Marxist analysis, precisely because some of them cannot afford longer periods without a job, they have to accept what is on offer—i.e. temporary jobs lacking social security, workplace protection, respect, and capacity to unionize.

What is true for the precariat is even truer for projectarians. In order to "make it" in the ultra-competitive artistic circulation one needs to commit to long years of unpaid or underpaid activities. After a financially demanding and long educational process, projectarians only enter into an endless cycle of internships (Precarious Workers Brigade 2011; 2017; BFAMFAPhD 2014). But even the more "mature" forms of "employment" in contemporary art are either unpaid or underpaid (W.A.G.E. 2010; Kozlowski, Sowa, and Szreder 2015). For example, artists or other content creators typically do not receive any—or only symbolic—payments for their activities. Even more fundamentally, as argued above, every projectarian needs to spend enormous amounts of time on securing opportunities, i.e. writing applications and competing for projects or jobs. Furthermore, it is notorious that only the execution phase of the project is paid, thus projectarians are expected to conduct research, make preparations and wrap up projects at their own expense. And only the most privileged (by inheritance or by happenstance) can afford to make it. Eventually, less affluent projectarians are fated to accept less prestigious jobs, as they are unable to compete for higher positions with their more privileged colleagues, an injustice covered by a semblance of meritocracy, an old trick in the playbook of class societies, thoroughly dissected by sociologists of social reproduction, such as Pierre Bourdieu (Bourdieu 1984). In these circumstances, UBI would become a grand equalizer of not only chances but also outcomes of social processes. In the artistic circulation, they tend to be indistinguishable from each other. A successful project opens up new opportunities, and a chain of those constitute a trajectory of "success." It also goes in reverse, an uneven start (due to inherited disfranchisement) results in less prestigious jobs that only drag people further down, limiting their chances for a major breakthrough or a "successful" career. In other words, injustice accumulates over time, creating stark inequalities that are detrimental to the vast majority of art workers. The UBI would help to break this vicious cycle.

Due to its egalitarian and universal thrust, the struggle for the UBI is set in direct opposition to the neoliberal ideology that legitimizes the inequalities as resulting from "natural" differences in merit (Phillips and Malik 2012), and reinforces the position of gate keepers as opportunity providers. According to this highly ideological discourse a metropolitan gallery does not exploit their interns, but offer amazing opportunities to skill up and gain a foothold in a vibrant industry (that holds true only for the most privileged). In this parallel universe, corporations are charitable benefactors, speculators become titans of the arts, unscrupulous profiteers are turned into venerable donors, all that to artwash tarnished reputations (Wu 2003; MTL Collective 2018; Penny 2019; Evans 2015).

One of the main functions of this hegemonic ideology is to not only justify the reproduction of privilege and resulting inequalities, but also to obfuscate the economic role played by what Gregory Sholette terms as artistic dark matter (Sholette 2011). He uses this apt, cosmological metaphor to discuss the architecture of the artistic universe, where a tiny elite is celebrated in a spotlight, whilst the gravity of this social world is maintained by the throngs of invisible, and yet indispensable artistic producers. Following Marx, Sholette not only debunks hierarchies in earnings and prestige, but also dissects systems of exploitation that keeps them in place. As he argues, the labor of the artistic multitudes—art students and aficionados, amateurs and professional artists, art handlers and facilitators, curators and educators—is indispensable for the artistic universe to function. And yet its role is deliberately negated by the hegemonic ideology that presents success in the arts as derivative of individual talent and/or effort, and not as a result of intersectional and multi-layered structures of exploitation and privilege. Considering the systemic relation between exploiters and exploited, the UBI is not an unwarranted charity, but rather a justified compensation for labor dutifully provided, which is socially necessary and yet unrecognized, underpaid and undervalued.

Interestingly, similar arguments were voiced by Boltanski and Chiapello already in the mid-1990s. In the *New Spirit of Capitalism* they argue for universal basic income to combat structural inequalities inherent to networked societies (Boltanski and Chiapello 2005). Networks—in order to function efficiently—always require dormant resources (incl. "human resources") that can be mobilized for various economic and social undertakings. Projects, in this arrangement, are temporary pockets of accumulation in an otherwise unstable world. The main advantage of such arrangement for project-initiators is that they do not have to pay for the reproduction of resources that are temporarily utilized. However, this situation is devastating for both human and non-human agents and their assemblages, who have to bear the brunt of accumulation, but do not benefit from its results. They are mere resources to be used by better-connected and more mobile others—be it a multinational corporation "investing" in one of deindustrialized towns of global rust belts, or a metropolitan curator on artistic safari in one of the peripheral countries. This tendency is only amplified by the structures of financial capitalism that captures the commonwealth generated by the dispersed, multifaceted labor of the multitudes, exploited by the means of credit, rent, and speculation (Hardt and Negri 2009; Marazzi 2010). Importantly, this situation is repeated in the artistic circulation, where individuals and institutions who accumulate economic, social, and cultural capital, exhort a disproportional chunk of the artistic commons generated by the dispersed labor of artistic projectariat. In more concrete terms, art celebrities typically benefit from trends, idioms and ideas not only of their own making, large biennales harness attention that is generated in dispersed networks of artistic producers and rely on their attendance to maintain their reputations, corporate museums exploit artists, interns and their own workers to sustain their global outreach.

This relationship between forced invisibility of various forms of labor and their economic undervaluation resembles the status of the care labor, often conducted by women and other carers, that—under capitalist relations of production—is deemed economically unproductive but sustains the economy as such (Federici 2012; Weeks 2011; Gibson-Graham and Dombroski 2020). To explain this structural conundrum feminist economists JK Gibson-Graham use an image of the iceberg, where a small tip of capitalist economy (dominated by wage labor, for-profit enterprise, and capitalist finance), hovers above a vast, but invisible, bulk of economic iceberg constituted by care labor, free exchange, barter, cooperatives, commons, and other non-capitalist forms of economic activity (Gibson-Graham 2006). Rendering them economically invisible, i.e. unaccountable for, enables their exploitation, as they are used as a freely available resource by agents operating at the pinnacle of capitalist economy. As we have argued with Kathrin Böhm in a visual essay *Icebergian Economies of Contemporary Art*, the relationship between artistic celebrities and artistic dark matter is structured in a similar manner, a small and highly visible group of individuals and institutions dominates over a vast, social mass of not-so-famous artistic producers and their initiatives (Böhm and Szreder 2020). Even though their labor and creative energies are indispensable for the reproduction of the entire structure, their input is undervalued, therefore easily exploited.

The UBI would change that by covering the costs of social reproduction, which are currently absorbed by artistic multitude, whilst curbing the excesses of the 1% by redirecting the flow of both economic resources and symbolic recognition (reputational imbalances result from social dominance, exhorted by more powerful on less affluent, the UBI would support truly horizontal, hence decentralized networks, enabling a multitude of alternative art worlds to thrive).

Towards the UBI or the class consciousness of the artistic projectariat

Hopefully, all that has been written above, explains why the UBI is so popular amongst radicalized fractions of the projectariat, and supports the argument for UBI as a remedy for some of the ills that they experience on a daily basis. However, instead of concluding the argument here, I would like to develop it further. Following Marx's 11th thesis on Feuerbach ("philosophers have hitherto only interpreted the world in various ways; the point is to change it"), let me ground the notion of the UBI in the social and political struggles of the projectariat. Implementing UBI on a global scale is a prospect as distant as a vision of international communism. However, I would argue that the very struggle for the UBI both requires and facilitates a transition of artistic projectariat from being a class in itself to becoming a class for itself (to use another old-school Marxist notion). In more straightforward terms: art workers would need to self-organize, unionize and establish lasting political alliances in order to contribute to the social transformation on the scale required to implement the UBI globally. The very process of unionization would in itself make a lasting impact on the ways of living and working endemic to the projectariat. Specifically, as argued above, it would undermine the hegemonic ideology that hinders their politicization by promoting individualistic atomization, cult of youthful enthusiasm, cynical entrepreneurialism and unrestrained mobility, which is beneficial only for a tiny, privileged elite.

In the struggle for UBI, projectarians would need to self-organize, countering a strong tendency for entrepreneurial self-precarization and cynical networking, which eradicate trust and undermine comradeship, but also leads to social exclusion and reproduction of artistic dark matter (it is a slippery slope from fame to obscurity). Patainstitutions, collectives, social movements, affinity groups create interdependent support structures that offer psychological and material help in times of need. They also create a sound basis from which projectarians can wage their struggles. This entrepreneurship of multitudes (Hardt and Negri 2017) would aim at reclaiming, establishing and protecting commons, countering the strong tendency for privatization.

For the vast majority of projectarians, in spite of the ultra-individualism characteristic to artistic circulation, privatization leads only to precarity and poverty. In the winner-takes-all-economy, of which contemporary art is a prime example, most people lose, while having to pay the costs of participation in the social game that is rigged against them from the very onset. The campaign for UBI is a counter-hegemonic struggle precisely because it debunks a pseudo-meritocratic pseudo-individualism of the artistic mainstream (I call it pseudo-individualism as it relies heavily on the reproduction of class, race, and gender privileges that are social constructs in the first instance).

Following this line of argument, to become advocates of the UBI art workers would need to undergo a process of politicization, interlinked with self-organization. They would need to dissect structural causes of their own misery, as directly related to the extractivist, neoliberal capitalism and hyper-inequality that underpins it. Furthermore, they would need allies—unions, movements, and parties—to transform them. Thus, they would need to debunk the ideas of artistic exceptionalism, understanding their own position as shared with other precarious people, that can be amended only as a result of major social struggle. Last but not least, they would need to become traitors of their own class and countries of origin. If the UBI is to be truly universal, it will require distributive schemes of climate and global justice. Consequently, the struggle for the UBI is in fact a struggle against virulent nationalism and fascism, crucial elements of the progressive politics overshadowed by the anti-immigrant sentiments and the grim reality of climate catastrophe.

Bibliography

Abbing, Hans. *Why Are Artists Poor?: The Exceptional Economy of the Arts*. Amsterdam: Amsterdam University Press, 2002.

Artdex. "Berlin Launches Its Grant Program to Help Artists and Freelancers during Coronavirus Lockdown." *Artdex* (blog), 2020. https://www.artdex.com/berlin-launches-its-grant-program-to-help-artists-and-freelancers-during-coronavirus-lockdown/.

Baravalle, Marco. "On the Biennale's Ruins? Inhabiting the Void, Covering the Distance." *Institute of Radical Imagination* (blog), May 2, 2020. https://instituteofradicalimagination.org/2020/05/02/on-the-biennales-ruins-inhabiting-the-void-covering-the-distance-by-marco-baravalle/.

Benjamin, Walter. "The Author as Producer." *New Left Review*, August 1970. http://www.newleftreview.org/?view=135.

Berardi, Franco. *The Soul at Work: From Alienation to Autonomy*. Los Angeles: Semiotext(e), 2009.

BFAMFAPhD. "Artists Report Back." New York: BFAMFAPhD, 2014.

Böhm, Kathrin, and Kuba Szreder. *Icebergian Economies of Contemporary Art*. 2020. https://www.pirammmida.life/cpe.

Boltanski, Luc, and Eve Chiapello. *The New Spirit of Capitalism*. London: Verso, 2005.

Bourdieu, Pierre. *Distinction: A Social Critique of the Judgement of Taste*. Translated by Richard Nice. London: Routledge, 1984.

Committee for the Radical Change in Culture. "Manifesto of the Committee for the Radical Change in Culture." *Variant*, October 15, 2009. http://www.variant.org.uk/37_38texts/1ed_2manifest.html.

De Carolis, Massimo. "Toward a Phenomenology of Opportunism." In *Radical Thought in Italy: A Potential Politics*, edited by Paolo Virno and Michael Hardt, 37–53. Minneapolis: University of Minnesota Press, 1996.

Evans, Mel. *Artwash: Big Oil and the Arts*. London: Pluto Press, 2015.

Federici, Silvia. *Revolution at Point Zero: Housework, Reproduction, and Feminist Struggle*. Oakland, CA: PM Press; Brooklyn, NY: Common Notions, Autonomedia; London: Turnaround [distributor], 2012.

Foucault, Michel. *The Government of Self and Others: Lectures at the Collège de France, 1982-1983*, edited by Arnold I. Davidson and Graham Burchell. New York: Picador, 2011.

Fraser, Andrea. "L'1%, c'est Moi." *Texte Zur Kunst* 83 (September 2011): 114–27.

Gibson-Graham, J.K., and Kelly Dombroski, eds. *The Handbook of Diverse Economies*. Northampton: Edward Elgar Publishing, 2020.

Gibson-Graham, J.K. *Postcapitalist Policies*. Minneapolis: University of Minnesota Press, 2006.

Gielen, Pascal. *Pascal Gielen: The Murmuring of the Artistic Multitude. Global Art, Memory and Post-Fordism*. Amsterdam: Valiz, 2009.

Hardt, Michael, and Antonio Negri. *Commonwealth*. Cambridge: Harvard University Press, 2009.

———. *Assembly*. New York: Oxford University Press, 2017.

Judah, Hettie. "Everyday Heroes: Key Workers Celebrated at Southbank, Where Hundreds Face Sack." *The Guardian*, September 2020. http://www.theguardian.com/artanddesign/2020/sep/03/everyday-heroes-review-key-workers-portraits-southbank-centre.

Kopel, Dana. "Against Artsploitaition." *The Baffler*, no. 59 (September 2021). https://thebaffler.com/salvos/against-artsploitation-kopel.

Kozlowski, Michal, Jan Sowa, and Kuba Szreder, eds. *The Art Factory*. Warsaw: Bęc Zmiana, 2015.

Kunst, Bojana. *Artist at Work, Proximity*

of Art and Capitalism. Winchester, UK; Washington, DC: Zero Books, 2015.

Lazzarato, Maurizio. "The Misfortunes of the 'Artistic Critique' and of Cultural Employment." In *Critique of Creativity: Precarity, Subjectivity and Resistance in the "Creative Industries,"* edited by Ulf Wuggenig, Gerald Raunig, and Gene Ray, 41–57. London: MayFly Books, 2011.

Lorey, Isabell. "State of Insecurity: Government of the Precarious." In *Futures*. London; New York: Verso, 2015.

Marazzi, Christian. *The Violence of Financial Capitalism*. Translated by Kristina Lebedeva. Los Angeles: Semiotext(e), 2010.

McRobbie, Angela. *Be Creative: Making a Living in the New Culture Industries*. Cambridge, UK; Malden, MA: Polity Press, 2015.

MTL Collective. "From Institutional Critique to Institutional Liberation? A Decolonial Perspective on the Crises of Contemporary Art." *October* 165 (Summer 2018): 192–227.

Penny, Daniel. "The Artist-Activists Decolonizing the Whitney Museum." *The Paris Review* (blog), March 22, 2019. https://www.theparisreview.org/blog/2019/03/22/the-artist-activists-decolonizing-the-whitney-museum/.

Phillips, Andrea, and Suhail Malik. "Tainted Love: Art's Ethos and Capitalization." In *Contemporary Art and Its Commercial Markets: A Report on Current Conditions and Future Scenarios*, edited by Maria Lind and Olav Velthuis, 209–43. Berlin; New York: Sternberg Press, 2012.

Precarious Workers Brigade. "Fragments Toward an Understanding of a Week That Changed Everything…" *E-Flux Journal*, 2011. http://www.e-flux.com/journal/fragments-toward-an-understanding-of-a-week-that-changed-everything%E2%80%A6/.

———. *Training for Exploitation? Politicising Employability and Reclaiming Education*. London; Leipzig; Los Angeles: Journal of Aesthetics & Protest Press, 2017.

Raunig, Gerald. "Factories of Knowledge, Industries of Creativity." *Semiotext(e) Intervention Series* 15. Los Angeles: Semiotext(e), 2013.

Ross, Andrew. *Nice Work If You Can Get It: Life and Labor in Precarious Times*. New York: New York University Press, 2009.

Sherwood, Harriet. "Unesco Warns of Crisis in Creative Sector with 10m Jobs Lost Due to Pandemic." *The Guardian*, February 8, 2022. https://www.theguardian.com/culture/2022/feb/08/unesco-warns-of-crisis-in-creative-sector-with-10m-jobs-lost-due-to-pandemic.

Sholette, Gregory. *Dark Matter: Art and Politics in the Age of Enterprise Culture*. London; New York: Pluto Press, 2011.

Standing, Guy. *The Precariat: The New Dangerous Class*. London; New York: Bloomsbury, 2014.

———. *Basic Income: And How We Can Make It Happen*. A Pelican Introduction 14. London: Pelican, an imprint of Penguin Books, 2017.

Steinhauer, Jillian. "A Crisis in Community Reach: MoMA's Arts Educators on the Consequences of Their Contract Cuts." *The Art Newspaper*, July 2020. http://www.theartnewspaper.com/analysis/moma-cuts-art-educators-amid-funding-squeeze.

Virno, Paolo. *A Grammar of the Multitude*. Los Angeles: Semiotext(e), 2004.

W.A.G.E. "W.A.G.E. Survey." New York: W.A.G.E., 2010.

Weeks, Kathi. *The Problem with Work: Feminism, Marxism, Antiwork Politics, and Postwork Imaginaries. A John Hope Franklin Center Book*. Durham, NC: Duke University Press, 2011.

Wu, Chin-Tao. *Privatising Culture*. London: Verso, 2003.

Smash the patriarchy: social reproduction and the invisibility of essential labor

Ilenia Caleo

[perceptions] *We are living exhausted presents which may be filled with possible futures.*

Sinking into the present to imagine possible futures addressing the (bodily, emotional) experience that we have and are living: the pandemic crisis which feminist movements highlight being both a health crisis and a "crisis of care." This experience impacts on our bodies focusing at the same time on the complex systems through which inequalities are being created and consolidated: in this context multiple factors related to our bodies, sexuality, identity and racialization combine to create new violent compounds. Yet, precisely in this context of crisis and weakening of social and relational links, new struggles on income have and are emerging often exactly from those same conditions of extreme precariousness and invisibility.

To keep together income struggles and transfeminist and decolonial demands is the indication we get from the future telling us about a new political and affective articulation of materiality.

[tool one] *The materiality by/in which we are suggests strategies to us.*

The point I want to start from is this renewed attention to materiality which we get in its multiple forms and temperatures from the most recent feminist thought because I believe that from it we can collect elements/knots to read and reimagine current scenarios.

A first useful concept-tool is that of active acting matter. My text of reference is *Vibrant Matter. A Political Ecology of Things* by Jane Bennett, where the philosopher proposed the idea of active matter to untie materiality from the constraint with inertia of what can be considered passive, not formed, heavy, opaque, mechanical matter which would need an external active principle that could, at the same time, animate it, give it shape and make it intelligible.

But what is *the use* of defending the vitality of matter? Why is it not just a merely theoretical thrust? This shift provides insights into feminist politics and opens up the prospect of new queer ecologies. The idea of dead, inert, passive matter may nourish and strengthen fantasies of conquest and domination. The idea that resources may be available for free is mirrored (a) on territories and natural resources where nature is conceived and described as outside of history; (b) on the bodies and on the free reproductive work done by women that, when naturalized, becomes like any other available resource. This narrative legitimizes a devaluation (Silvia Federici) which we *must* read in parallel. The extractivist model is constitutively *also* a paradigm of domination and consumption, exploitation and violence, intimately connected to the colony system and to the division of sexual work.

With Haraway, Bennett, Barad, and other new materialism thinkers it is possible to recognize other forces besides human forces, other powers being not only forces of resistance, negative forces, forces of friction, but also fully productive forces acting in the shared space, the public space. Learn to imagine them.

[crack] *Also, ghosts haunting us are material.*
Is art, in particular the scene, the place where invisible forces can be made visible? Can it be acted upon by bodies other than human? What are the bodies acting on the art scene and on the public scene? What dramaturgies and choreographies are there for not only human bodies and affects? We need new figurations/imaginations/new aesthetics in the sense of new articulations of the sensible to provide body and futurity to those openings.

Smash the patriarchy:
social reproduction and the
invisibility of essential labor

[tool two] *We want to think world-nature without producing pacified scenarios.*

Conflict. It is politically necessary to produce a non-pacified version in rethinking nature culture: the idea of active and acting matter is to be thought of as a continuous production of difference, not of homogeneity. Vitalism and monism of a Spinozian matrix do not go towards the undifferentiated, they rather equate to the continuous production of differences, of ways, of forms, of intensity and therefore of movement, of collisions, of disturbances and perturbations (Bennett, Serres), of the forces that are at stake; of the relations of those forces and therefore—also—of their asymmetries.

That's how the gaze on materiality thus focuses on the dimension of the conflict and must help us identify new and specific areas of conflict, new maps for political action. A post-anthropocentric generic statement is not sufficient. What's needed is a complex articulation of materiality, of the economies of exchange, of the interrelationships generating material conditions of life/of the many lives at stake.

[variation] *Out of control.*
This vibrating activity of matter—one may call it its productive independence—has one more characteristic: *it escapes our control*. This applies to natural, geological, and meteorological forces, as well as to the assemblages between human and non-human objects: hurricanes, ecological disasters, garbage and waste, toxic and radioactive substances, pollutants, and pharmaceutical products.

Two examples: *Toxic bodies* (a), *The hurricane* (b).
(a) *Toxic bodies.* In the perspective of a political ecology, bodies and environment are irreversibly entangled and the actions occurring in their interactions/intra-actions are neither defin-

able nor controllable. On the proliferative capacity of materials, Turkish theorist Serpil Opperman writes "We all dwell in a world crisscrossed by deviant agencies that now populate the Earth. Since these xenobiotic forces and substances have the power to reshape bodies and disrupt physical environments, we must pay close attention to their often-unpredictable agentic dimension. Agency manifests in many ways, and even in garbage."

(b) *The hurricane.* In *Political Affect. Connecting the Social and the Somatic*, John Protevi analyzes Katrina as a destructive assembly of human and non-human forces and shows how far a series of interrelated factors could exponentially enhance a hurricane's—as "a natural phenomenon"—catastrophic effects: the weather and geological conditions, the erosion of the coast in the last twenty years, the destruction of coastal flora, the intensive exploitation of the Mississippi water basin and the consequent perturbation of its nearby ecosystems, together with the colonial and slave history of the city which nowadays still imprints New Orleans urban planning, real estate speculation against social housing, the organization of rescue operations, and the fear of black riots in memory of the many also in its colonial past—often obliterated episodes of resistance. Protevi maintains that a racial (and racist) component played a decisive role in the management of the emergency: the aid's heavy militarization, fearing revolt by African American groups—the most violently affected by the hurricane—basically stopped the self-organization and solidarity resources which had already been autonomously activated by the local population before aid arrival.

{A vision: Spike Lee's documentary *When the levees broke* (2006)}.

An event that is "a set of natural and social elements," a dramaturgy of forces that summons different *dramatis personae*: the River, the Wind, the Sun, the Sea, the Coast, the Intensive

Cultivation, the racialized population of New Orleans, the Revolts, the Work, the Slave Trade, the City, the Ghetto, the Fear, the Plantation. Protevi returns us the ecological dimension of the political body through an ecosystemic-affective-materialistic lens: to explain this event referring to the participation of linear contributing causes is not enough. It is also necessary to gather the *multidimensional entanglement* simultaneously moving on different time levels, on active temporalities: from the very long and more-than-human time of the geological transformations, to the historical time of the colony (in Anna L. Tsing this model is in and of itself an *era*, the Plantationocene corresponding to: entanglement of the intensive monoculture model + exploitation of labor + 16th century labor and crops interchangeability + scalability + the segmented and fragmented plot model); from the time of sedimentation of affects presiding over a community's identity, to the istantant time of the emergency military government. All of these diffracted temporalities react on a stratified urban map made of ghettos and enclaves. A reading impacting also on methodologies through which we look at history and change, precisely considering the different forces at play.

The object hurricane is this space-time tangle, an object whose edges cannot be defined clearly, which remains blurred and fluctuating. A new type of object (Morton). When talking about colliding materialities, materialities that enter into conflict, the relationship with Spinoza's philosophy gets revitalized, restored by Deleuze and feminist thought. Spinoza also invites us to think about the combinations between bodies being not always positive, not always "joyful."

There are positive assemblies (like bacteria in our gut) and negative assemblies (when eating poisonous mushrooms). As such, the virus, the pandemic, and other catastrophes are all unhappy human/non-human assemblages.

Ilenia Caleo

[crack] *The virus is a body-between-bodies, an "unexpected subject."*

It is about rejecting the metaphors of war, of the enemy, of immunity as military defense of bodies, in order to name and to face the socio-sanitary consequences of the virus. On the contrary, by adopting a transfeminist gaze, during these months of pandemic we began to feel in a very concrete way, and to focus on the widespread condition of interdependence—of the bodies, the subjects and the causes among one another. One other way to name it is transcorporeality (Alaimo). It may seem intuitive and self-evident to recognize where one body ends and another body begins, the inside and outside of living beings, be it the skin, the surface or the exoskeleton. Yet in recent months the Covid-19 virus challenged the concept of the hermetic and self-sufficient body—it is a body among other bodies; it is tiny, invisible, yet it acts. It invites us (forces us) to think not by individual bodies, but by transcorporeality, by complex and interrelated systems. Bodies are not sealed or separate—we are always composite bodies made up of many other bodies. We already are inhabited by other foreign alien bodies that pass through us. Transcorporeality thus becomes a concept laboratory helping us to imagine new systems of alliances/mixtures even among social bodies.

In this deeply interrelated context in which reciprocity of traffic and exchanges are made (because risky) so concrete by the pandemic, we as a small group of artists—performing art workers—together with the all the other workers began to visualize that no corporate defense, and no claim of an alleged exceptionality of artistic work, can be effective. Very inspiring for us are the struggles that have taken place in other sectors like logistics, care, and sex work. "Not for us but for everyone" is the slogan of the riders that we made our own to counter the corporate claims of separate statutes, and the consolidation of privileges and positions that always run the risk of becoming dominant in the artistic and cultural work sector, especially in the situation of lack of rights and recognition, exacerbated by the pandemic. To also point out that there is no opposition between wage struggles and unconditional income struggles. Interdependence is therefore a trace that signals possible political practices, reactivating submerged genealogies, and interlacing different struggles.

[perceptions] *We are not all equal before the virus.*
Some bodies are already compromised, more vulnerable, more exposed, more tired, more exhausted. There are some subjects that more than others are invisibilized. Suddenly the quality of homes and living, food, income, as well as the access to full citizenship—upon which also the access to care and the health systems depend—have become visible elements, and have taken center stage in public discourse in Italy as it hasn't happened for years. Also, the jobs (and their subjects) involved in, and connected to, the activities of care and social reproduction have become more visible.

This virus is rather egalitarian, yet it does not bring us all under the same conditions. The degree of health and well-being of the bodies, their exposure and vulnerability, is strongly influenced by social determinants. This emerges during the pandemic, during natural disasters or during the environmental crisis. We all have seen how extremely hard Hurricane Katrina hit New Orleans' black population. The same lesson we learned during the AIDS pandemic. In the same way as Bolsonaro's health policies turned into a selective genocide of black, indigenous and poor people.

Thus the virus draws a map of vulnerabilities and returns all the violence of the inequalities produced by the multiple factors at play. At the same time this map also indicates to us the possible unforeseen alliances, networks, and interdependencies among subjects that can become political. Interdependencies which—if recognized, named and consolidated—can help us trace the contours of bottom-up welfare infrastructures and social mutualism.

[a practice] *Re-create the Globe.*
So how could artists react? We have two possibilities: either to affirm the exceptional nature of artistic work, claiming its separate statute, thus reaffirming the patriarchal myth of the artist as separate from the world; or to fully feel ourselves part of this interrelated world and translate this perception into social terms. Indeed, thinking of the art sector as a space for experimenting with new models and extensible prototypes/*not for us but for everyone.* After all, contemporary work increasingly assumes traits and characteristics that had been peculiar to artistic work, as it is infiltrated by its linguistic, relational and affective dimension.

And there is more. Those areas are far from pure. Cultural work as a whole is highly fragmented, and everybody's income is the result of a set of composite economies: working as bar attendant or as waiter, providing training in various fields (in informal schools or workshops), working as technician, rider, dj, janitor, or working in clubs and in the nightlife economies, and also tutoring, translating, teaching yoga, combining it with different research jobs. Ultimately: adding up an infinite amount of shit jobs, all of them precarious jobs, that even if put together, do not make a whole. Only a few—by fortunate circumstances or by class privilege—can devote themselves entirely to cultural work and make a living from it. Defining oneself as an "artist" often results from the concealment of these spurious identities we cross. What

Smash the patriarchy:
social reproduction and the
invisibility of essential labor

sense would it make to claim for a professional register or an exceptionality of art that does not exist in reality? Each one already embodies and crosses multiple relational and working systems, multiple specific knowledges, multiple professional "identities," multiple precarious conditions, after all not so different among them. To politically translate these systems of co-dependence—and at the same time to make the effort to disidentify from any "pure" professional identity making invisible these self-exploitation and blackmail mechanisms is one of the plans we have addressed within *Il Campo Innocente*—an informal collective/an assemblage of fagot, non-binary, lesbian, queer, trans people, artists, cultural workers, women—born in 2019 in the wave of queer and #NUM transfeminist movements.

The name we chose in and of itself is a statement: *Art Is Not An Innocent Field*, meaning it is no neutral space, it is no safe space. Even in the art world there is sexism, violence, machismo, racism, homolesbobitransphobia, discrimination just as within the social movements and the struggles. Art is not a world apart, it needs de-romanticizing and depatriarchalizing. In the midst of the pandemic for five days in April 2022 in Rome we occupied the Globe Theater together with the self-organized trade union networks RISP (Rete Intersindacale Professionisti dello Spettacolo) and other performing arts workers, all converging on the request for unconditional income and the recognition of intermittences. Commonalities were born in this roofless open-air theater, among riders, school workers, and the laborers movement. This is where the work and discussions around the *Art for UBI (manifesto)* spilled out.

We opened a workshop based on our direct experiences of the relationship between sexism and precariousness.

As women/non-binary/fags/trans/disabled people putting into play our own bodies, our whole emotional sphere, our

Ilenia Caleo

whole imagination, often we are more exposed to ambiguous, problematic, violent situations. Power dynamics, toxic and abusive contexts are connected to and strengthened by precariousness. The more precarious we are, the more exposed, fragile, blackmailable we are. Autonomy and self-determination are linked.

We thought a lot about how to collectively be able to say "NO." This is the reason why we came to understand it is only by having the possibility to refuse—to say no—that we can avoid blackmail.

> "Am I allowed to refuse a job, when the context is toxic? When the demand for performativity is excessive? When I am asked to push my body to the limit to constantly work? Can abuse be legitimized in the name of art? Is violence always evident? Why do I always have to be in warrior mode? How much energy and effort does it cost me? Is discomfort a symptom? What are the boundaries of my workplace? Have you ever felt [or told you are] too thin/too fat? Or too 'feminine'/too little 'feminine'? Too young/too old? Are you allowed to touch my ass in the name of artistic freedom or contact improvisation?"

These are some of the questions that emerged over the months and which have gradually come to form campaigns, speeches, moments of exchange and self-training or self-inquiry informal sessions. In this context, income—without conditionality and outside a familist and patriarchal matrix—represents not only a response to precariousness, but also and more profoundly a way out of violence. Income brings us out from the blackmail to work at all costs, the costs being life, health, psycho-physical and sexual well-being, or happiness. This perspective leads us to a double movement, an unstable yet necessary transit to give substance to the struggles of the future.

Smash the patriarchy:
social reproduction and the
invisibility of essential labor

The focus on income and the material conditions of existence is also necessary for transfeminist struggles to avoid the shift we have seen in recent years—in our feminist collectives, in queer spaces—towards an emotional turn of the struggles (Dorlin), an unpolitical withdrawal from internal conflict, a fetishization of trauma and cover up of class dimension within the politics of identity.

Yet there is no going back from the advancements the most recent transfeminist movements produced: to speak of income and material conditions in a disembodied way—without taking into account the violence, the asymmetries linked to bodies, gender and sex, or the racialization processes—is but an abstraction reproducing a patriarchal and colonial model. Precarity is no neutral universal: within queer and feminist communities, networks of relationships and new intimacies are already experimental and advanced forms of mutualism to draw inspiration from.

Reference readings

Alaimo, Stacy. "Trans-corporeal Feminisms and the Ethical Space of Nature." In *Material Feminisms*, edited by Stacy Alaimo and Susan Hekman. Bloomington: Indiana University Press, 2008.

Bennett, Jane. *Vibrant Matter. A Political Ecology of Things*. Durham: Duke University Press, 2010.

Barad, Karen. "Posthumanist Performativity: Toward an Understanding of How Matter Comes to Matter." *Journal of Women in Culture and Society* 28, no. 3 (2003).

Deleuze, Gilles. *Che cosa può un corpo? Lezioni su Spinoza*. Verona: Ombre Corte, 2007.

Dorlin, Elsa. *Se défendre: Une philosophie de la violence*. Paris: Édition La Découverte, 2017.

Frost, Samantha. "The Implications of the New Materialisms for Feminist Epistemology." In *Feminist Epistemology and Philosophy of Science*, edited by Heidi E. Grasswick, 69–83. Berlin: Springer, 2011.

Hird, Mira. "Naturally Queer." *Feminist Theory* 5, no. 1 (2005).

Morton, Timothy. *Hyperobjects. Philosophy and Ecology after the End of the World*. Minneapolis: University of Minnesota Press, 2003.

Oppermann, Serpil. "Toxic bodies and alien agencies. Ecocritical perspectives on ecological others." In *The Postcolonial World*, edited by Jyotsna G. Singh and David D. Kim, 419. New York: Routledge, 2017.

———. "Il corpo tossico dell'altro. Contaminazioni ambientali e alterità ecologiche." In *ContaminAzioni ecologiche. Cibi, nature e culture*, curated by Daniela Fargione and Serenella Iovino. Milan: LED Edizioni Universitarie di Lettere Economia Diritto, 2015.

Protevi, John. *Political Affect. Connecting the Social and the Somatic*. Minneapolis: University of Minnesota Press, 2009.

Serres, Michel. *Lucrezio e l'origine della fisica*. Palermo: Sellerio, 2000.

Spinoza, Baruch. *Etica. Dimostrata con Metodo Geometrico* (1677), edited by Emilia Giancotti. Rome: Editori Riuniti, 1988.

Tsing, Anna L. *The Mushroom at the End of the World: On the Possibility of Life in Capitalist Ruins*. Princeton: Princeton University Press, 2015.

*Questioning UBI
through the lens of care*

*Maddalena Fragnito and
Raising Care Assembly*

About the Raising Care Assembly

Raising Care is a platform that brings together people who struggle to redistribute care within and beyond their collectives. Born during the pandemic within the framework of *The School of Mutation* activated by the *Institute of Radical Imagination*. In September 2021, as part of the programme *On the Precipice of Time: Practices of Insurgent Imagination. The Zapatista Forum*, we've articulated *¡Cuidados!* a workshop on care that took place at the autonomous space La Villana de Vallekas. The aim is collecting knowledge and urges of communities: healthcare access support, housing struggles, reproductive justice, care workers' rights. This workshop contributed to straightening the alliances between collectives and biosindicates from Spain, Greece, Serbia and Italy, merging their experiences and the tools they developed. The common starting point is conceiving care as an act of constitutive resistance, to question how to co-design a better world for the most starting from now. To activate group dynamics we designed a fanzine as a collaborative methodological tool to open up new questions, rather than to offer answers. A tool to think with all those who are imagining different social and ecological possibilities. A selection of four questions included in the zine are presented in this article.

WHAT ARE WE CARING FOR?

Questioning UBI
through the lens of care

In the recent months, the lexicon of care has become ubiquitous in activists analyses and practices, as well as in every discourse of governments, digital platforms and private companies. However, care labor has always been at the centre of all relations between humans and non-humans on the planet. What gets saved and what doesn't, who is able to live and who can only afford to survive, are decisions at the heart of every assemblage and society, historically formalized by different models of care re/distribution. One may say the organization of care creates societies' necropolitical assumptions. From this perspective, the same Covid-19 pandemic can be read as a crisis highlighting many of these assumptions, such as the division between who received healthcare and who did not, or the social composition of who bore the heaviest burden of care labor needed.

To ask "What are we caring for?" aims at making the possibility of different models of care re/distribution visible, starting by recognizing the divergence between the anthropocentric, racial and patriarchal capitalist model of care organization, and the conflicts opened up on the terrain of eco-social reproduction by heterogeneous subjectivities. On the one side, we have the model where social and ecological reproduction tasks have never been acknowledged as work, rather, have been ascribed to the sphere of "natural" resources to make them available for appropriation and to legitimize the immense extortion of wealth. On the other side, all conflicts moved against the exploitation of communities, common lands and resources; against the precarious care labor working conditions; against police and governments' violence. We can consider those conflicts as care work: their actions are at the same time a form of labor to survive the capitalist model of care that kills, and a practical indication of different ways of considering and organizing the planet's limited social and ecological resources.

Every decision on the terrain of care implies making decisions about the life and death of what surrounds us and who we are. Thus, making visible the conflict at stake is the way to collectivize those decisions. *What is essential, and what is not, and for whom?* are crucial political matters still delegated to few governors. During the *Raising Care* assembly—an alliance of collectives struggling for the recognition of care rights and care as labor—when confronted with this situation, an important question arose from inspecting practices of solidarity emerged during the first year of the pandemics: *How can we accelerate the shift from "care as an individual task," mostly rooted to a domestic domain, to "care as the basis for the construction of collective processes" to sustain life?* (Raising Care 2020). To socialize this question means to collectively rethink what is to continue re/producing, and what is no longer worth re/producing. To refuse to perform care labor that permits capital re/production is thus a practice involving a collective consideration on what is no longer worth living for, to improve the conditions of life itself.

The socialization of these processes of re/valuation uncovers the political character of care as "a neuralgic zone of conflict" (Molinier 2019). Thus, care is nothing intrinsically "natural," nor "nice" or "maternal," rather it is about the struggles against the current necropolitical management of lives. To prefigurate more equitable living assemblages, the organization of care is the main ground of conflict.

WHO CARES FOR THE CARERS?

*Questioning UBI
through the lens of care*

One must disinvest the self-sufficient subject fantasy, to acknowledge that care labor is denied and devalued work, traditionally excluded from the spheres of politics and economics. It is the sphere the capitalist model has thrived upon exploiting low- or no-paid, feminized, and racialized workforce, transforming bodies and ecosystems into mere resources to exploit.

The division between productive and reproductive activities—i.e. those within the market and those suspended in an extra-economic space—derive from Greek thought. Plato and Aristotle began to divide the world, relations and human beings into opposing categories: superior/inferior, spirit/body, theory/practice, culture/matter, male/female, master/slave, public/private, and so on. The reduction of economics to what is monetizable is based upon this original dichotomy, and as a consequence bodily materiality and needs have been considered an annoying obstacle for the freedom of the spirit, thus removed to a lower sphere where other bodies are forced to take care of it: all workforce socialized to internalize the duty of care is considered a mere deposit of unlimited resources to be exploited. This separation is the cause for a part of the population to believe to be independent of the others, having no need for or necessity of/to care. From this perspective, even if care concerns everyone, some dominant subjects of modernity—mainly white men—have and continue to enjoy the privilege of delegating care tasks to others. The division of labor into bodies entitled to good health and rest, and those whose health does not matter, and who are not entitled to rest (Vergès 2019), shows how the world of economy systematically loses sight of half of what's defined as "human needs satisfaction." Thus, to reduce the space of economy only to what is exchanged and monetized, distances this science from what it should be born about (Praetorius 2019).

Decades of neoliberalism exaggerated the self-sufficient subject fantasy, exalting individual capacity for self-expansion, within the logic of productivity, where all changes in rhythm are interpreted as an obstacle—i.e. childhood, oldness, sickness, disabled and neurodivergent people—making dependency a pang of guilt and a source of humiliation. Figures are clear. In 1980 the UN published the results of a study: "while women represent 50 per cent of the world's adult population and one third of the official labor force, they perform nearly two thirds of all working hours, receive only one tenth of the world income, and own less than one per cent of world property." In 2019, Oxfam's *Time to Care* report claimed that, on a global scale, the value of unpaid care work done by women aged 15 and over, is equivalent to at least $10.8 trillion a year. To make the figure less abstract, it is the equivalent to three times the monetary value of the world's technology industry. According to the annual OECD Reports on global living conditions, women work more than men, when both paid and unpaid work (e.g. routine housework and care work for children and adults) are taken into account, and in the worst conditions (2020). In Madrid in 2021 during *¡Cuidados!* workshop by the Institute of Radical Imagination, *Territorio Doméstico* collective states: *"We should have the right to decide for our own care: we want to decide who takes care of us and how."* The collective is based in Madrid and is part of the *Transborder Biosindicate*, a network of political organizations to give dignity to essential care labor, to enable life worth living for.

ARE ALL CARE NEEDS MEASURABLE?

*Questioning UBI
through the lens of care*

In recent years, the proposal for a Universal Basic Income (UBI) has made its way through academia, policymakers and on the field experimentations in territories and cities. The idea is to decouple pay from work performance. Through the taxation of large profits, this proposal would entail the redistribution of wealth, unconditional sustainability for all, and a greater economic autonomy, particularly for those who are regularly excluded from wages. It can also enhance self-determination in work choices allowing the possibility to say "NO" to some "shit jobs" (Graeber 2018).

During the pandemic, another proposal gained momentum, the *Universal Basic Services* (UBS). The proposal focuses on the need for strengthening the public services, such as healthcare, housing, transportation, and education. Even though UBS was born as opposed to UBI, some ideas it carries are crucial. UBS theories criticize the UBI approach for relying only on money as a form of redistribution and thus for not taking into account some of the limitations that could arise from this approach. For instance, if public services were privatized, no agreed basic income could ever be sufficient. Feminist collective *La Laboratoria* writes, "if you have good public services, you have no need to work long hours. If you have decent access to public housing without having to pay for huge rents, you are not forced to accept no matter what working conditions. If you are not forced into debt at the end of the month, you are not going to accept no matter what working condition" (2020).

As a transversal thread of the *Raising Care* assemblies, this claim appears at the basis of the debates around labor rights, support networks, and ecologies of care: *"How can we make care a public good? How do we socialize care?"* This question is put at the centre by *Obiezione Respinta* and *Mesa de Mayores* collectives, who are fighting to introduce the socialization of care inside healthcare policies. The same attempt is carried on by the *Open School for Immigrants of Piraeus* in the field of public and solidarity education.

UBS also brings to the forefront of the debate the issues of consumption and production. By identifying the network of public services and the ways to access basic needs, the UBS proposal intends to promote a form of public and shared consumption, rather than a private and individual one. UBS aim "is to achieve security and justice for all, now and in the future; the challenge is to identify these limits [between a social base and a green roof] and to consider how they might be realized in practice" (2020). Thus "feminists will have to combine demands for public services, demands for basic income and demands for bottom-up design of technologies that serve the needs of households and communities rather than those of big business" (Ursula Huws 2019).

To sum up, UBS's substantial contribution includes the ecological perspective as one of issues for social transformation. A weakness in UBS' proposal may lie in the fact e that it provides for targeted, and not for universal measures, i.e. most of the time it opens up complicated discussions about who may be entitled to access basic services, and who may not. The fundamental aspect brought by the UBI model instead, lies precisely in stopping dividing people into target groups, and stop transforming all our relationships into evaluation systems. In other words: *"How do you measure the time spent not doing anything at all, in order to open a space for thinking differently?"* (2018).

HOW TO SOCIALISE CARE LOGICS?

*Questioning UBI
through the lens of care*

Often UBI and UBS are articulated as alternative or opposing proposals, from the perspective of care it would be more convenient to combine the two together. In this line of thought we open a third speculative proposal: the "Unconditional Planetary Livability" (UPL!), combining the desire for self-determination that underlies the UBI proposal, with the enhancement of social infrastructure and the reduction of global consumption implied in the UBS proposal. In UPL: "Livability" stands for the urgency of defining our existence between plausible margins of sustainability, and the material need for public and common services; "Planetary" is in opposition to the false myth of universalism, by rethinking the enlarged *milieu* of interdependence among humans, non-humans, animals and lands; finally, "Unconditional" stands for the radical exercise of trust that the proposal for UBI has placed at the centre, rejecting any division among human beings, and any obscene desire for cheap and false metric's system solutions.

The radical transformation of what is understood today as economics is a call to revert priorities: to move away from the market exchange as organized and conceived by capitalism, and move towards the satisfaction of human and non-human fundamental need to preserve the quality of life and life itself. A call for such transformation comes from different territories of the world: the "Jineolojî" science (founded by the Kurdish women's movement in 2012; the "Buen Vivir" paradigm of the Abya Yala tradition;[1] the "Gross National Happiness" introduced in the Bhutan Constitution in 2008; the definition of "dignity of the creature" introduced in the Swiss Constitution in 1992. Moreover, the many books and manifestos recently published by activists, communities and researchers, are all together calling for a society centred on the extended concept and visibility of care for the living. From all these attempts, voices and practices, a new question generates: *As assemblages of non- and living entities, what activities do we need, and what can we do without?* In other words, it is about making a choice concerning what is no longer worth keeping alive in order to improve the very conditions of life.

---

1 These alternative societal constructs are expressed in the constitutions of Ecuador (2008) and Bolivia (2009) through concepts such as Buen Vivir, Sumak Kawsay (Kichwa) and Suma Qamaña (Aymara). There are similar notions among diverse indigenous people, such as the Mapuche (Chile and Argentina), the Guarani (Paraguay, Brazil, Argentina and Bolivia) and the Kuna (Panama and Colombia). This worldview is also found in the Mayan tradition in Guatemala and among the diverse indigenous groups that inhabit Chiapas in Mexico. Beyond Abya Yala, there are many other inclusive philosophies across the world, which, in one way or another, are related to the search for living well, or *buen vivir*. This includes the concept of Ubuntu in Africa and Svadeshi, Swaraj and Apargrama in India.

This question generates new forms of refusal of all work that reproduces further socio-ecological destruction: from stopping fixing the effects of capitalism, to the resignation from useless jobs. Indeed, caring does not mean reproducing the same, rather undoing worlds and relationships, transforming them so that other worlds and other relationships—perhaps more habitable—can emerge.

Maddalena Fragnito and
Raising Care Assembly

Reference readings

Al-Ali, Nadje, and Isabel Käser. "Beyond Feminism? Jineolojî and the Kurdish Women's Freedom Movement." In *Politics & Gender* 18, no. 1 (March 2022): 212–243. Cambridge, UK: Cambridge University Press (online). November 20, 2020. https://www.cambridge.org/core/journals/politics-and-gender/article/abs/beyond-feminism-jineoloji-and-the-kurdish-womens-freedom-movement/540F612294D931881942FA74EB5F7C61.

Coote, Anna. "Universal basic services and sustainable consumption," *Sustainability: Science, Practice and Policy*, December 23, 2020. https://www.tandfonline.com/doi/full/10.1080/15487733.2020.1843854.

Fragnito, Maddalena. "Per una vivibilità planetaria incondizionata." *Euronomade*, 2021. http://www.euronomade.info/?p=14485.

Graeber, David. *Bullshit Jobs: A theory*. New York: Simon & Schuster, 2018.

Government of Bhutan, *The Constitution of the Kingdom of Bhutan Art 9.2.* (October 30, 2019). Retrieved October 19, 2010. https://www.nationalcouncil.bt/assets/uploads/files/Constitution%20%20of%20Bhutan%20English.pdf.

Huws, Ursula. "The hassle of housework: digitalisation and the commodification of domestic labour." *Feminist Review* 123 (2019): 8–23. Thousand Oaks, CA: SAGE Publications.

Joy, Elieen A. "'An Instrument for Adoration': A Mini-Manifesto Against Metrics for the Humanities (to be Elaborated Upon at a Later Date)." In *Human Metrics / Metrics Noir*. Coventry: Post Office Press, Rope Press and meson press, 2018.

Lawson, Max, Anam Parvez Butt, Rowan Harvey, Diana Sarosi, Clare Coffey, Kim Piaget, and Julie Thekkudan. "Time to care. Unpaid and underpaid care work and the global inequality crisis." *Oxfam International*, January 20, 2020.

Praetorius, Ina. *L'economia è cura. Una vita buona per tutti: dall'economia delle merci alla società dei bisogni e delle relazioni*. Milan: Altreconomia, 2019.

OECD. *How's Life? 2020: Measuring Well-being*. Paris: OECD Statistics and Data Directorate, March 2020.

Raising Care Online Assemblies. *Care for people*. November 2020. https://instituteofradicalimagination.org/2020/10/18/raising-care-care-for-people/.

RRS Radio Museo Reina Sofia. *El feminismo sindicalista que viene*, produced by Maria Andueza. May 2021. https://radio.museoreinasofia.es/feminismo-sindicalista-que-viene?fbclid=IwAR1ziCATWiWGcdkAYpQP1e3K0XgupS07QEEJnpTBeOhlm2EDk6lo-4RUd_c.

UN. *World Conference of the United Nations Decade for Women: Equality, Development and Peace, Copenhagen, 14 to 30 July 1980: report*. New York: United Nations Publication, 1980.

Toomey, James. "Constitutionalizing nature's law: dignity and the regulation of biotechnology in Switzerland." *Journal of Law and the Biosciences* 7, no. 1 (January–June 2020), lsaa072, https://doi.org/10.1093/jlb/lsaa072.

Vergès, Françoise. *Un féminisme décolonial*. Paris: La Fabrique, 2019.

A Pluriversal Basic Income [1]

Gabriela Cabaña and Julio Linares

[1] The following is a fragment of the unpublished *Towards an Ecology of Care: Basic Income Beyond the Nation-state* written by Julio Linares and Gabriela Cabaña. A full length book is coming in the future.

Introduction

In this piece, we argue for a Basic Income that decouples wage slavery from people's time in order to bring forth a social ecological just world. We argue that the ethical and moral imperative of basic income is that we, as inhabitants of the planet, should not have to pay in order to exist in it. Recentering our awareness of care as the source of the value in our actions can be achieved through the emergence of a Basic Income given to people just because they exist. Epistemically, the following formulation of Basic Income offers a different basis from current nation-state basic income proposals through a critical re-appraisal of our current money form, which can serve as a tool for the emergence of new political-economic projects and social forms beyond the current capital-state nexus: the pluriverse. Politically, the pluriverse is a weaving together of different forms of knowing, imaginations and practices of freedom organized democratically as a confederation in order to transcend the nation-state universalism and support in the creation of a world where many worlds can live, from the local to the planetary. Economically, a pluriversal basic income is a means of practicing economic democracy via the anti-imperialist and anti-colonial re-organization of current capitalist supply chains into ecological lines.

Recovering care as a precondition for freedom

Bringing care to the core of our thinking requires a deep questioning of the way in which the discipline of economics has built its object ("the economy"). Most of the sub-schools in the field of economics tend to treat the work of care—by some conceptualized as social reproduction—as invisible, making it a valueless and unaccounted form of labor. This labor is treated as pre-economical and is therefore not measured in metrics like GDP. Today, this care or reproductive labor is socially assigned predominantly to women. It is made invisible through a hierarchy of value which dualistically divides between some forms of labor as material (and hence productive) and others as immaterial (and hence communicative or "feminine") and through the coloniality of power, which constructs only certain bodies as valuable while others are categorized as sub-human and exploited for the purposes of capitalist accumulation (Yanagisako 2012; Bear, Ho, Tsing and Yanagisako 2015; Quijano 2011).

This is not a casual theoretical mistake. The invisibilization of reproductive work completely decenters the processes that make human life possible by putting them outside the sphere of what is considered as part of the economy. But in fact, what we call production is only a secondary moment in the process of social reproduction, or the production of people (Graeber 2013). Any economy is fundamentally a human economy, and it is only by invisibilizing things like reproductive work that capitalism can justify its costs of production and pretend that the economy is about things and not social relations (Hart and Laville 2010; Federici 2014).

In reality, the freedom of the proletariat to sell their labor is only possible because of the unfreedom of the housewife which subsidizes their reproduction for eventual capitalist exploitation (Mies 1998). As some note, the level of freedom in a society can be measured by the level of freedom that women have (Öcalan 2015). Hence, without the systemic liberation of women and all others who perform the basis upon which life is built, and therefore the reproduction and defense of the commons, society as a whole cannot be liberated. The exploitation of those mainly dedicated to care is the material counterpart of the theoretical overlooking of this form of labor.

It is through fostering and encouraging the recognition of care work as a source of value in work that another world can be built: a care centered economy (Praetorious 2015). This implies a shift from valuing the end point of things, as done under capitalism, to a valuing of the processes that make life possible to begin with.

An economy based on care, or the care economy, is a response to capitalist and patriarchal systems of domination. The care economy tries to recenter the value of care labor (as these reproductive activities have come to be known) at the center of the human economy, or rather, an ecology for human relations that is strengthened through their interdependence. Thus, the reproduction of human processes is the first step and precondition for the production of what is known under capitalism as the production of "goods and services."

Underpinning this economy is an ethics of care, a moral system which recognizes the interdependence amongst humans and their capacity to autonomously decide which relations they wish to enter, change or exit. Most importantly, it is based on the experience of being cared for and the giving of care. At its core, an ethics of care is about "attending to and meeting the needs of the particular others for whom we take responsibility" (Held 2006).

With this in mind, we can think of an ecology of care as the soil that nourishes human relationships directed at mutually making each other free through an acknowledgement of our interdependence and the care that goes into making us who we are. Care is therefore a precondition for free relationships to be established. As argued below, this type of morality and system of value is embedded within a reformulation of how our tokens of value are created; shifting to a system which provides every human being with an amount of money necessary to live in harmony with the rest of nature and within planetary boundaries: the pluriverse.

Money, Basic Income and the Critique of Capital:
But where will the money come from?

Money is a new form of slavery, and distinguishable from
the old simply by the fact that it is impersonal—that there is no
human relation between master and slave.   Leo Tolstoy

The circuit of capital, identified by Marx's formula M-C-M' denotes the fact that, under the capitalist mode of production, money begets more money through the exchange of commodities (Marx 1982 [1894]). These are produced through a mixture of humanity's labor power and nature i.e. the means of production, all mediated by the circulation of value in the form of money, given as an interest-bearing debt.

Monetary creation under capitalism is the ignitor and precondition for economic growth mainly because only the principal is issued out as a debt while the interest can only come from people increasingly competing in labor markets in order to repay back their loans. Capitalist debt money is the fuel that mobilizes the expansion of future production with the sole goal of profit maximization. The endless expansion of economic growth using this type of money creation leads inevitably to ecological disaster, as enclosures on land and people's labor power become the means of money's infinite reproduction, making wealth inevitably accumulate at the top 1%, as recent studies have demonstrated (Robbins 2018; Piketty 2013).

Ecological destruction and the rising of entropy in the planet thus happens initially through the issuance of interest-bearing debt, which makes money scarce and hence competitive for people to obtain, tying humanity's fate with an expansive spiral of destructive growth. Some economists have empirically demonstrated that monetary interest rates set by central banks follow and are positively correlated with GDP growth. Bank credit creation not only mobilizes future production but is the basis for economic growth (Werner 2016; Werner and Lee 2018). As evidence is increasingly demonstrating, we cannot have infinite growth on a finite planet (Meadows, 1972; Hickel and Kallis 2019; Hickel 2019).

More recently, feminist autonomous Marxist intellectuals like Silvia Federici, among many others, have traced the historical changes in the circuit of social reproduction and its relationship to the circuit of capital, namely women's historical central function in the process of primitive accumulation as the producers and reproducers of the most essential capitalist commodity: human labor power (Dalla Costa and James 1975; Federici 2014; Praetorious 2015). The enclosure of the commons and of women's bodies was the pre-condition for the rise of capitalism. As historian Peter Linebaugh puts it: "reproduction precedes social production. Touch the women, touch the rock" (Linebaugh 2008).

The rebuilding of the commons as a viable political project has been defined and practiced dispersedly around the world. This essay on the pluriverse is an attempt to deepen the imagination of the economic self-reliance of the commons. As Federici herself notes, talking about the recent appropriation of the commons discourse by hegemonic forces:

While international institutions have learned to make commons functional to the market, how commons can become the foundation of a non-capitalist economy is a question still unanswered (Federici 2011).

The idea of Basic Income, without having been implemented fully in any nation-state, has stimulated the political imagination of a wide political spectrum (Standing 2017). More than engaging in creative solutions of how we could redistribute diverse funds for a Basic Income, we propose instead to unpack current understandings of the monetary system and its underpinning

Gabriela Cabaña and
Julio Linares

institutions to formulate politically relevant questions about the nature of the system itself and the wider social forms it reproduces today, in order to create new ones. What is money? How is it created? What institutions does it uphold? How could a different money system help to bring forth a different world?

Money is Debt and Debts are Promises

From the archeological record, we know that money historically emerges in human civilization from our social relationships of debt. Underpinned by violence and mathematics, the creation of debt has been employed throughout history as a mechanism of enslaving human beings, from ancient Sumeria to today's International Monetary Fund and World Bank (Hudson 2004).

The history of debt is a history of patriarchy, defined here broadly as the rule of fathers. The long imperial hegemonic structures which underpin this logic of domination, the long durée of money, have remained roughly the same for the past 5,000 years, going through different oscillations.[2] Traditionally, kings and bureaucrat priests who had power over the hegemonic ideology would pair up with armies in order to enslave people into becoming their subjects through debt (Graeber 2011; Öcalan 2015). This 5,000 year old pattern has been reproduced to today's Federal Reserve, Wall Street, underpinned by the violence of the US army.

---

2   Anthropology has countless examples of what some call "socialcurrencies," which are aimed at rearranging social relations as a means rather than the mere movement of commodities for the sake of the capital accumulation as an end in itself. Just as markets are not the same thing as capitalism, money does not necessarily imply capitalism and can thus be transformed.

3   Money as a commodity is how most people and schools of thought, including orthodox Marxists, defined it up until now. The aversion towards money is prescient in most leftist circles as it is equated with capitalism and slavery and hence is seen as something rotten which should be abolished. Against this, we follow the view that money is always utopic (Dodd 2014) and we should therefore appropriate monetary institutions within the realm of the commons, making it multiple, a plurality. For the commonification of money, see the next section.

This *phenomena* could be described as the Military-Coinage-Slavery complex; whereby a king would hire an army in order to subject people to his command, enslave them and make them work in order to pay the wages of soldiers in newly issued money (Graeber 2011: 229; Ingham 2004: 99). This complex continues to exist until today, with elite groups in private banks having the privilege over monetary creation, making everybody else indebted and enforcing payment through state violence. Banks are thus the temples of today, where the debts of the many get accumulated by the few. Knowing its history, the question remains: what is money?

Economic textbooks define money as a neutral thing: a means of exchange, a store of value and a unit of account. This formulation assumes that money, to exist as such, has to achieve all of those three characteristics, with people often arguing about each of these as what makes money "really" money to begin with. In reality, these are the functions of money, what it does, not what money *is* (Lietaer 2002; Lietaer and Dunne 2013).

If money is debt, then debts would be a series of promises we make to one another (Graeber 2001; 2011). As a mutual promise between people, money is not just one thing but is fundamentally a social convention or an agreement, a semantic system akin to language we all agree upon and use, underpinned by the trust people give to it (Aristotle 1954; Polanyi 1977: 97–119).

This acknowledgement of debts as mutual promise is based on an arrangement that recognizes our interdependence to other people, which is constantly renewed and revised. It is a recovery of money fundamentally as a social process before a commodity-like thing (Simmel 2004; Dodd 2014). Money is a social relation of debt and credit between people, a process and a thing *at the same time* which guides the whole of what we call "the economy" (Hart 1986).[3]

But the way that money works today follows a logic of domination that goes against the natural yield of biological systems to reproduce themselves. This is because money can infinitely make more money through arbitrary compound positive interest bearing loans issued as bank deposits, which necessarily implies some form of material resource extraction somewhere down the line, however much alienated from it the issuer is. Historically, we know there is nothing natural about adding positive interest rates to debts between people.[4] Those who possess money and reproduce these cycles of accumulation often take the ability of those with none of it to reproduce their livelihood; through the repayment of debts, wage-slavery, rent and interest rates, money's relationship to human beings has been, for the most part of the last 5,000 years history, one of domination and exploitation.

Modern colonial money is produced in the form of debt by private and central banks, which often do not use it to mobilize production but to speculate in financial markets. In that sense, finance, defined as other people's debts, are really the imagination of capitalism (Haiven 2011), as it allows for the future promises of capitalism to continue its exploitation. Today, 97% of all the money supply in most countries is produced in the form of bank deposits issued by private banks. The remaining 3% is produced by states in the form of cash (Mcleay et al. 2014). These institutions both produce money out of thin air, by merely typing a number on a computer screen.[5]

There is no fortuity in this. The so-called divine power once used by temples and priests to create something out of nothing today rests in the hands of private bankers, who issue money as debt, and ultimately with nation-states, whose sovereignty guarantees that they can perpetually issue promises without having to pay them back, as modern monetary theory (MMT) proponents have argued, synthesizing both state and credit theories of money (Mitchell–Innes 1914; Knapp 1924).

Ultimately, to understand money we need to understand debt and through this understanding we can begin to decolonize its very constitution. In German, *schuld* is the word for both debt and guilt.[6] This "demonic ambiguity" as Walter Benjamin called it, is why money has such a powerful effect on human beings (Benjamin 1996). According to Benjamin, it is the internalized feeling of the morality of guilt in our current patriarchal human civilization which underpins the current agreement of how capitalism is organized, from the origins of patriarchy to early Christianity, to the Protestant work ethic (Weber 2001), to today's so-called "post" modern world. This feeling of guilt over who owes what to whom is an embodied expression of power and ultimately what reproduces the moral economy of debt which capitalism is based upon. How do we begin to decolonize debt?

Decolonizing Money: A Pluriversal Basic Income.

In our dreams we have seen another world, an honest world, a world decidedly more fair than the one in which we now live. We saw that in this world there was no need for armies; peace, justice and liberty were so common that no one talked about them as far-off concepts, but as things such as bread, birds, air, water, like book and voice. Subcomandante Marcos

A Pluriversal Basic Income (PBI) is a common promise that can be issued and claimed by communities who politically

---

4 In fact, interest rates have shifted according to various religious and philosophical traditions, from the famous Saint Ambrosio exception in the Middle Ages which stated that a Christian cannot charge an interest on another person's time, to Calvin and Luther who argued that, in fact, you can. See Graeber (2011) for a detailed analysis of this history.
5 The latin word fiat is used today to denote the type of money made by nation-states: fiat money. The term can be found in Genesis 1.3.— "let there be light" or fiat lux—denoting the making of something out of nothing.
6 For an archeological study of the biblical usages of sin and debt and the jubilee year, see Hudson (2018).

decide to share and appropriate wealth in order to live free and equal lives, building alternatives to the cosmology of capitalism and the nation-state.

This formulation of a Basic Income is epistemologically differs from nation-state proposals, as it aims to go beyond and within our current social forms to weave a pluriverse outside of it (Kothari et al. 2019). The pluriverse here serves as a practical and conceptual tool to overcome the homogenization of reality made by the violent social relations of capitalist modernity that has brought about the destruction of our ability to understand the world in all its diversity (Öcalan 2015).

The pluriverse is an embodied alternative which goes against the modernizing logic of the nation-state, in that it does not create a separation between the subject and the object but instead looks at reality as one interconnected diverse whole, where the past and the future are contained in the impermanent present (Rivera Cusicanqui 2019).

According to anarchist Silvia Rivera Cusicanqui, the pluriversal "indigenization" of the world is a recognition that all languages are in fact indigenous languages from the communities in which they emerge from. But as Rivera Cusicanqui stresses, colonialism has a very specific usage for words: they encover instead of designating what things are. History is filled with countless examples of double-think and double-binds, where the meaning of words is twisted in order to control and dominate others.

If we think of money as a semantic system akin to language, a series of promises which carry values and meaning about the

---

7   Social ecologists speak of first nature as non-human nature and second nature as an emergent property of life in the form of human consciousness and society. At a systemic level, money today is one of the links that ties first nature to second nature together in a hierarchical relation which must be severed and made anew. See Bookchin (1982).

8   We base this on the already-existing organizational practices and systems of communal indigenous government in Latin America, confederated systems based on direct-democracy in the Middle East and elsewhere. See, for example, Leyva Xochitl et al. (2008); Silvia Rivera Cusicanqui (2015: 17); Boaventura de Sousa Santos et al. (2018: 127); Ashish Kothari et al. (2019: 151).

world we live in and our collective memory, it becomes clear that the fiction of money being a commodity and not a promise is what reproduces the colonization of the planet (Hart 2001; Polanyi 1944; Zelizer 1997). This must be questioned.

To decolonize money we need epistemes that recognizes that people are all part of nature before they are anything else, interconnected and interdependent to the whole.[7] This decolonization practice aims at understanding the roots of our individual and collective trauma through money.

Decolonizing money is an exercise at healing the internal colonialism of our experiences and our relationship to money and the bureaucratic institutions that underpin it. Through the decolonization of debt, we can undo the guilt it produces in people's bodies, which stops people from relating to others. After all, the so-called economy which money animates is itself an interdependent mesh of relationships however colonized they are. To turn guilt into responsibility and into the love and struggle for life is to decolonize the debts that bind us together as a common project of action. To decolonize money it to begin making these promises anew. Basic Income is a means to making new promises to each other and to the world.

Some people say that the emancipatory value of a Basic Income is higher than its monetary value (Standing 2017). The gradual introduction of this new basic income money aims at challenging the long standing guilt over our debts, work and wealth, through its equal, abundant and unconditional predistribution.

A basic income which transcends the nation-state boundaries is therefore an attempt at reformulating the relationships we have with each other and with the world. It is different in the sense that it is constituted democratically as a political plural entity with the potentiality to encompass all human beings in a planetary federation.[8]

Gabriela Cabaña and
Julio Linares

This pluriversal basic income is a share of the wealth of the collective and it only becomes basic once people can meet their basic livelihood needs such as care, food and housing, which in turn is inherently embedded with the reproduction of the commons, understood in their holistic sense. A pluriversal basic income is thus a gradual reappropriation of wealth from capitalism to the commons.

The social form any given society takes is marked by its monetary institutions. These institutions are responsible for allocating the means of production (land, labor, capital) and ultimately determine what value is through the circulation of currency, whatever its form. The monetary institutions of the day are a remnant of enlightenment rationality and do not reflect current understandings in the field of complexity science, chaos theory or even quantum physics.

The positivist banking structures of today have the monopoly over society's trust to issue credit. This privilege produces a centralized and fragile monetary structure which creates a scarcity of money and a vacuum for the extraction of value.

The complexity of the money system can no longer be managed by a patriarchal central planning committee. The decentralization of the production of money as a credit or money commons, organized democratically by all who use it, would create more resilient and ecological circuits that go beyond the binarism of nation-states and their globalized financial institutions.

A relocation of the position of where the promises are issued from, would mean the transformation of how value is produced, defined and distributed. The more people issue promises to each other in communal ways, the more we can begin to free each other from the promises of the State.

Currently, the nation-state is the sovereign of money, the ultimate backup of promises based on fear and violence. If we want to reclaim the control of money, we need to change how it is produced; through the reformulation of the principle of sovereignty in human organization. Whether the decentralization of sovereignty, its transformation as a pluriversal autonomous zone, a planetary commons or its total abolition as a principle of domination; the imagination required to change the sovereignty of nation-states today is deeply tied together through money and the violence it upholds.

Money as a promise means that the *fiction* of the nation must continue to exist in the near future. Otherwise, the money would not be worth anything. In a way, it is the very threat of violence that gives future value to nation-state money. This is what creates and upholds our current universalism and what we must transcend if we wish to co-create an internationalist alternative.

Embedding money into the pluriverse means to start creating institutions which embody the diversity of the world without commodifying it. Basic Income resolves the modern-colonial contradiction between freedom and equality, as everyone has the freedom to say no to relations of domination by having an equal ground to stand on.

Basic Income thus allows people to be both free and equal in their diversity. A monetary pluriverse forms the basis for a democratic confederation of political imaginations, living in harmony with one another and with the world. It is a plural union of what we are and the identities that capture our individual and collective stories. All respecting each region with its own democratic control over its own autonomous forms of production, distribution, exchange and consumption, where power is seen and embodied by all, distributed equally and negotiated through democratic assemblies.

A Planetary Income
A pluriversal, planetary basic income would then be an unconditional amount of money issued by all human beings on the

planet. A planetary income necessarily needs a planetary politics, rooted in local anti-imperialist struggles—a paradigm shift from current nation-state politics, where wealth is democratized and administered by people in confederated assemblies, from the local, to the regional, to the planetary.

A planetary income is the recognition of our interdependency to the whole and to each other, a promise to upheld our interdependence. It aims at emerging from capitalist modernity through the reshaping of the tokens of value that fetichize the definitions of our wealth, our agreements with each other and their corresponding institutions.

The pluriverse sets the stage for a fundamental break from the patriarchal systems of sovereignty, which include by excluding *the other* into its formulation of the self and its cosmic-polities (Sahlins 2017). Instead, the pluriverse tries to weave the different epistemes in order to understand the impermanence of reality in its different emergent levels and let the polity emerge from there (Kothari et al. 2019).

In this way we can ease the death of the world as we know it and lay at rest the ashes of the old. As the Zapatistas and other groups often remind us, the world has ended many times before. We must accept that. Once we do, we will realize that the phoenix representing the rebirth of another world is ever more near.

Conclusion: The Commonification of Care and the Decolonization of Money

The current form of money has been a fundamental tool of colonial projects. Moving to a pluriversal ecology of care would allow us to decolonise money. This decolonization would mean a change of what value is, where it comes from and where it stays. It is a means of changing the political categories of the day to ones that embody the will of the masses through the parallel and gradual redistribution of wealth. The decolonization of money is therefore the political ecological struggle over the definition of what value means as a common human project. This political deliberation necessarily implies a direct-democratic break from the representative bureaucracies of capitalist modernity.

In sum, a Pluriversal Basic Income (PBI) would enhance care in two ways: democratizing the possibilities of giving and receiving care, as people would be free and equal to decide what they want to spent their time on, and giving more space to the political debate on how to better care for one another.

For PBI to succeed in the ultimate goal of making people freer, it must rethink both the nature of money and the destructive logic of growth that is deeply inscribed in our global economic system. If Basic Income is about taking care of people, then it must be created and managed bottom-up, to avoid the extraction of value from the financial institutions that rely on money for accumulation and do not care for the "real economy."

This transformation of money would also allow us to question and rebuild our political institutions. The sovereignty of millions is bought and sold every day by the institutions that control the flow of money. Without properly addressing the question of the production of money, or who controls the creation of humanity's future promises, any revolutionary project which aims at changing the system is doomed to failure.

Without dis-embedding money from capital and the state, the enclosure of the commons will continue until full collapse. An acknowledgement of our systemic crisis requires a *reconstitution* of value, money and wealth, and not just their redistribution.

This call is not about the commodification of care, but the *commonification* or commonalisation, following De Angelis

(2007; 2017) of care. The decolonial money produced for the goal of taking care of people will make an unconditional basic income. There is no better time than the present to bring down the walls of our political imagination and bring a pluriversal basic income into being.

Bibliography

Aristotle. "The Nicomachean ethics of Aristotle." In *The World's classics*, 546. London: Oxford University Press, 1954.

Bear, Laura, Karen Ho, Anna Tsing, and Sylvia Yanagisako. "Gens: A Feminist Manifesto for the Study of Capitalism." In *Theorizing the Contemporary, Cultural Anthropology. Fieldsights*, March 30, 2015. Accessed July 10, 2019. http://www.culanth.org/eldsights/652-gens-a-feminist-manifesto-for-the-study-of-capitalism.

Benjamin, Walter. "Capitalism as Religion." In *Selected Writings* 1, edited by. C. Gödde and H. Lonitz, 288–91. Frankfurt am Main: Suhrkamp, 1996.

Bookchin, Murray. *The Ecology of Freedom: The Emergence and Dissolution of Hierarchy*. Palo Alto, CA: Cheshire Books, 1982.

Quijano, Aires. "Colonialidad del poder y clasificación social." In *Contextualizaciones Latinoamericanas* 3 (2011): 1–33.

Dalla Costa, Mariarosa, and James Selma. *The Power of Women and the Subversion of the Community*. Bristol: Falling Wall Press, 1975.

De Angelis, Massimo. *The Beginning of History: Value Struggles and Global Capital*. London: Pluto Press, 2007.

_____. *Omnia Sunt Communia: On The Commons and the Transformation to Postcapitalism*. London: Zed Books, 2017.

Dodd, Nigel. *The Social Life of Money*. New Jersey: Princeton University Press, 2014.

Federici, Silvia. "Feminism and the Politics of The Commons." *The wealth of the commons*, 2011. www.commoner.org.uk/?p=113.

_____. *Caliban and the witch: women, the body and primitive accumulation*. Brooklyn, NY: Autonomedia, 2014.

Graeber, David. *Toward an Anthropological Theory of Value: The False Coin of our Dreams*. Basingstoke, UK: Palgrave Macmillan, 2001.

_____. *Debt: The First 5000 years*. Brooklyn, NY; London: Melville House Publishing, 2011.

_____. "It is value that brings universes into being." In *Hau* 3, no. 2 (2012): 219–244.

Haiven, Max. "Finance as Capital's Imagination? Reimagining Value and Culture in an Age of Fictitious Capital and Crisis." In *Social Text* 29, no. 3 (2011): 108. Durham, NC: Duke University Press.

Hart, Keith. "Heads or Tails? Two sides of the Coin." *Man* 21 (New Series), no. 4 (1986): 637–656.

_____. *Money in an Unequal World: Keith Hart and his Memory Bank*. London: Texere, 2001.

Hart, Keith, Jean-Louis Laville et al. *The Human Economy*. Cambridge, UK: Polity Press, 2010.

Held, Virginia. *The Ethics of Care: Personal, Political, Global*. London: Oxford University Press, 2006.

Hickel, Jason. "Degrowth: A theory of radical abundance." *Real-World Economics Review*, no. 87 (2019): 54–68.

Hickel, Jason, and Kallis, Giorgos. "Is Green Growth Possible?" *New Political Economy* 25, no. 4 (2019): 1–18. https://doi.org/10.1080/13563467.2019.1598964.

Hudson, Michael. "The Archeology of Money: Debt versus Barter Theories of Money's Origins." *Credit and State Theories of Money*, edited by A. Mitchell Innes and L. Randall Wray, 99–127. Cheltenham, UK: Edward Elgar Publishing, 2004.

_____. *...And forgive them their debts: Lending, Foreclosure and Redemption From Bronze Age Finance to the Jubilee Year*. Glashütte, DE: ISLET-Vergal Dresden, 2018.

Ingham, Geoffrey. *The Nature of Money*. Cambridge, UK: Polity Press, 2004.

Knapp, George Friedrich. *The State Theory of Money*. London: Macmillan, 1924.

Kothari, Ashish, Ariel Salleh, Arturo Escobar, Federico Demaria, and Alberto Acosta, eds. *Pluriverse: A Post-Development Dictionary*. New Delhi: Tulika Books, 2019.

Lietaer, Bernard. *The Future of Money: Creating New Wealth, Work and a Wiser World*. Boulder, CO: Qiterra Press, 2002.

Lietaer, Bernard, and Jacqui Dunne. *Rethinking Money: How New Currencies Turn Scarcity Into Prosperity*. San Francisco, CA: Brett Koehler Publishers, 2013.

Linebaugh, Peter. *The Magna Carta Manifesto: Liberties and Commons for All*. Berkeley, CA: University of California Press, 2008.

Marx, Karl. *Capital Volume III*. Harmondsworth, UK: Penguin Classics, 1982.

McLeay, Michael, Amar Radia, and Ryland Thomas. "Money creation in the modern economy." *Bank of England Quarterly Bulletin* 54, no. 1 (2014): 14–27.

Meadows, Donatella et al. *The Limits to Growth; A Report for the Club of Rome's Project on the Predicament of Mankind*. New York: Universe Books, 1972.

Mies, Maria. *Patriarchy and accumulation on a world scale: women in the international division of labour*. London: Zed Books, 1998.

Mitchell-Innes, Alfred. "The Credit Theory of Money." In *Credit and State Theories of Money*, edited by A. Mitchell Innes, L. Randall Wray, 50–78. Cheltenham, UK: Edward Elgar Publishing, 1914.

Öcalan, Abdullah. *Civilization: The Age of Masked Gods and Disguised Kings – Manifesto for a Democratic Civilization: Volume 1*. International Initiative Edition, Norway: New Compass Press, 2015.

Piketty, Thomas. *Capital in the Twenty First Century*. Translated by Arthur Goldhammer. Cambridge, US: Harvard University Press, 2013.

Polanyi, Karl. *The Great Transformation*. Boston: Beacon Press, 1944.

———. *The Livelihood of Man*. New York: Academic Press Inc., 1977.

Praetorius, Ina. "The Care Centered Economy: Rediscovering what has been Taken for Granted." In *Publication Series Economy + Social Issues* 16, edited by Heinrich Böll Foundation. 2015.

Rivera Cusicanqui, Silvia. *Sociología de la Imagen: Miradas Ch'ixi desde la Historia Andina*. Buenos Aires: Tinta Limón, 2015.

———. "Ch'ixinakax utxiwa: A reflection on the practices and discourses of decolonization." *Language, Culture and Society* 1, no. 1 (2019): 106–119. Amsterdam, John Benjamins Publishing Company.

Robbins, Richard. H. "An anthropological contribution to rethinking the relationship between money, debt, and economic growth." *Focaal* 2018, no. 81 (2018): 99–120. https://doi.org/10.3167/fcl.2018.810108.

Sahlins, Marshall. "The Original Political Society." *Hau Journal of Ethnographic Theory* 7, no. 2 (2017): 91–128.

Simmel, Georg. *The Philosophy of Money: Third Enlarged Edition*. London: Routledge, 2004.

Sousa Santos, Boaventura, et al. *Epistemologías del Sur – Epistemologias do Sul*. Coímbra: Centro de Estudos Sociais – CES; Buenos Aires: CLACSO, 2018.

Standing, Guy. *Basic income: And how we can make it happen*. London: Pelican, 2017.

Weber, Max. *The Protestant Work Ethic and the Spirit of Capitalism*. London: Routledge, 2001.

Werner, Richard. "A lost century in Economics: Three theories of banking and the conclusive evidence." *International Review of Financial Analysis* 46 (2016): 361–379.

Werner, Richard, and Kang-Soek Lee. "Reconsidering Monetary Policy: An

Empirical Examination of the Relationship Between Interest Rates and Nominal GDP Growth in the U.S., U.K., Germany and Japan." *Ecological Economics* 146 (2018): 26–34.

Xochitl, Leyva, Araceli Burguete, and Shannon Speed, eds. *Gobernar (en) la diversidad: experiencias indígenas desde América Latina: Hacia la investigación de co-labor*. Mexico: CIESAS, Flacso Ecuador y Flacso Guatemala, 2008.

Yanagisako, Sylvia. "Immaterial and Industrial Labor: On False Binaries in Hardt and Negri's Trilogy." In *Focaal* 64 (2012): 16–23.

Zelizer, Viviana A. *The Social Meaning of Money: Pin money, Paychecks, Poor Relief, and Other Currencies*. Princeton, NJ: Princeton University Press, 1997.

*Financing the Many Worlds:
Pedagogies of (Il)liquidity*

Erik Bordeleau

Who renders whom capable of what, and at what price, borne by whom? Donna Haraway, *Staying with the Trouble*

Us the living, we are a minority. A provisional minority.
Jorge Luis Borges

The implementation of wealth redistribution schemes such as a Universal Basic Income (UBI) poses a series of complex political and design challenges. But one thing is for sure: the lack of resources is not one of them. There is actually plenty for everyone—if only we manage to properly articulate collective claims on the already circulating and vastly unjustly accumulated wealth.

Capitalism is an injustice-compounding machine that must be reprogrammed. But it seems like our traditional battery of political concepts and antagonistic practices isn't quite allowing us to rise up to the challenge. For Robert Meister, a political philosopher who is teaching in the department of History of Consciousness at USC Santa Cruz alongside Donna Haraway and Anna Tsing among other illustrious colleagues, and who is the author of the seminal *Justice Is an Option: A Democratic Theory of Finance for the 21st Century* (University of Chicago Press, 2020), the operational starting point to reprogram capitalism is to be encountered at the very heart of the techno-social machinery by which current wealth is preserved and accumulated, that is: finance. To be truly effective, argues Meister, any conceivable remedy for historical injustice must also be expressible, at least initially, *in the language that the financial sector uses to value its own abundance today*. "Justice can be made more present, more embodied, more actionable in the temporalities of the present," writes Meister as he evokes his fruitful collaboration with Randy Martin, "if it is recaptured conceptually through a new social and political understanding of the manufacture and pricing of *options* and not simply posed as the conventional radical demand for publicly financed and administered social programs."[1] This will be our starting point.

Adopting the language and conceptual framework of financial theory to address issues of compounding historical injustice starts with understanding finance as *a technology to manufacture liquidity*. Liquidity is a highly ambiguous and fleeting concept. As with many other things in finance, it is also highly self-referential. Liquidity corresponds to the ease with which an asset can be converted into money at a given market price. Or in other words, it describes the degree to which an asset or security can be quickly bought or sold in the market without affecting the asset's price. If something can be predictably sold at a certain price without having an excessive impact on the price of other related assets, then it means that there is liquidity.[2]

Liquidity, then, can be understood as a *promise of reversibility*. The investor brings her money to the market, under the condition that she can take it back whenever she wants. Liquidity is the other face of trust, or rather the peculiar type of trust that must reign in financial markets for them to be

---

1   Robert Meister, *Justice Is an Option: A Democratic Theory of Finance for the 21st Century* (Chicago: University of Chicago Press, 2020), 12 (slightly modified version based on a previous version of the manuscript).
2   "Market liquidity refers to the extent to which a market, such as a country's stock market or a city's real estate market, allows assets to be bought and sold at stable prices. Cash is considered the most liquid asset, while real estate, fine art and collectibles are all relatively illiquid." https://www.investopedia.com/terms/l/liquidity.asp.
3   Quoted in Massimo Amato and Luca Fantacci, *The End of Finance* (Cambridge: Polity Press, 2012), 16.
4   John Maynard Keynes, *The General Theory of Employment, Interest and Money*. https://www.marxists.org/reference/subject/economics/keynes/general-theory/ch12.htm. The passage continues: "Conversely, from the standpoint of the financial community and hence of investors en bloc—that is, from the standpoint of their consolidated balance sheet—investments are not liquid, since that would presuppose the liquidation of all economic assets in which financial capital is invested."

effective. Confidence makes the market liquid and liquidity makes the market confident. Or in the words of Jim O'Neill, from Goldman Sachs: "Liquidity is there until it is not— that is the reality of modern markets."[3] Many of the financial innovations we've seen in recent years aim at increasing the liquidity of the market, transforming private debtor-creditor relations into something that exists publicly and can be bought by a third party. This operation is called *securitization*, and by some historical irony that should not evade our scrutiny, it is closely associated with a steep augmentation of budgets for private security services. This fact highlights something about the (anti)social nature of liquidity that John Maynard Keynes noted already in 1936:

"*Of the maxims of orthodox finance none, surely, is more anti-social than the fetish of liquidity*, the doctrine that it is a positive virtue on the part of investment institutions to concentrate their resources upon the holding of 'liquid' securities. It forgets that *there is no such thing as liquidity of investment for the community as a whole.*"[4] (my emphasis)

Global wealth, that is, the cumulative value of the world's assets, cannot be accumulated in financial form without also remaining liquid. That's the *raison d'être* of financial options and derivatives. Wealth must keep on moving. *Liquidity must go on.* This is the name of the financial game. In this sense, Meister suggests, we need to conceive of liquidity as the abstract form of absolute power of financial capitalism. This abstract relational imperative becomes particularly crucial when considering the massive bail outs put in place during the financial crisis of 2008, but also, more recently, following the beginning of the COVID pandemic in Spring 2020 (which was roughly 3/4 times bigger than the 2008 one) to restore trust in the credit market. Without these massive financial interventions, the financial markets would have crashed, precipitating a series of blockages or *illiquidity events* of almost inimaginable magnitude. In both cases, and Meister is adamant on this point, States have insured the liquidity of capital markets *for free*, i.e., without requiring what he calls a *liquidity premium*. In an insurance contract, the risk is transferred from the insured to the insurer. For taking this risk, the insurer charges an amount called the premium. In the case of the bail out of 2008 and 2020, the governments have insured liquidity on the markets without any premium, that is, without making any specific claim on the upside of the recovery. Meister's analysis leads to an unmistakable conclusion: "I believe that the production of liquidity should be the focus of socialism— that liquidity is not free, that it's not a positive externality, that it is something for which a political price can be extracted."[5] In other words, preserving accumulated wealth in the form of financial assets has a price. And technically speaking, this price is that of the liquidity premium that should be requested by the States when they bail out the capital markets. This is the price of *justice as a (financial) option*.[6]

Meister is keen to point out how political these financial interventions are in effect. Quoting Roosevelt's brain-truster Adolf Berle, he writes:

> "'Any investigation of liquidity is a study of the mechanisms which make particular forms of wealth *acceptable*.' This implies, as Berle goes on to explain, that the political unacceptability of a particular form of wealth would preclude state support for its liquidity, and thus its convertibility into money and all the things that money can buy."[7]

The issue of how liquidity is guaranteed in current capital markets by democratic States is thus a highly political one, yet one that, for different reasons, we struggle to address fully as such. And more importantly, for the purpose of this volume, it also represents one key perspective on how to envisage the macro-financing of something like a UBI or some other justice-oriented wealth redistribution program.[8] But if the manufacturing of liquidity depends on how everyone of us is used as a collateral in complex financial arrangements and thus truly is, at the end of the day, a question of social and political acceptability, doesn't it make it even more attractive—and even more so, necessary—to simply *occupy everything*, that is, to put to a (definitive) halt this whole slick and abstract financial machinery and the logistical apparatuses it depends on, thus triggering a cascade of ever-amplifying illiquidity events? This question brings us back to another

---

5 https://democracyparadox.com/2021/10/12/robert-meister-believes-justice-is-an-option/.

6 The actual sum of the liquidity premium, according to Meister's own estimates, would have been, for the bailout of 2008, just short of the equivalent of that year's GDP, i.e. around 9 to 13 billions. In proportion, it is generally understood that the 2008 bailout was worth around 1 trillion for the United States alone (experts don't agree on what exactly should be included or not in this astronomical sum). Estimates for the 2020 COVID induced total stimulus package for the US varies from 3 to 4 trillions, while the whole world combines for an amount north of 10 trillions (and counting), according to the infamous consultant firm McKinsey: https://www.mckinsey.com/featured-insights/coronavirus-leading-through-the-crisis/charting-the-path-to-the-next-normal/total-stimulus-for-the-covid-19-crisis-already-triple-that-for-the-entire-2008-09-recession.

These numbers need to be taken with a grain of salt—I'm only providing them to give a sense of the magnitude of these unprecedented financial interventions. To be clear: the issue here isn't about the amounts themselves, but about how and who they benefit in the first place. For an informative overview on the world's global wealth and the what it is made of, I can only recommend this most pedagogical diagram provided by Visual capitalist: https://www.visualcapitalist.com/all-of-the-worlds-money-and-markets-in-one-visualization-2020/.

7 Robert Meister, *Justice Is an Option: A Democratic Theory of Finance for the 21st Century*, 139.

8 "Put very crudely, it seems to me that the collective demand for money—neither wages nor credit, but simply money as a redistribution of wealth—could be disruptive of the financial system in the sense of *making a common claim on the publicly created and guaranteed collateral that is used to secure accumulated wealth that remains in private hands*" (emphasis added). Robert Meister, "Liquidity," in *Derivatives and the Wealth of Societies*, eds. Benjamin Lee and Randy Martin (Chicago: Chicago University Press, 2016), 173.

one, stemming from the incandescent core of Occupy Wall Street and which remains largely unanswered to this day: *how to occupy a (financial) abstraction?*

Meister directly addresses the problem of what he frames as "the payoff of the revolutionary option" in these terms:

"For the purpose of funding justice, the most difficult abstract question is what the payoff of the revolutionary option would be. The ideal of revolutionary abundance assumes the accumulated wealth would be preserved intact despite its redistribution. In contrast, the ideal of revolutionary asceticism assumes that it shouldn't matter if accumulated wealth would lose all its value by being redistributed, since this would only prove that it was never real. *The truth is that we don't know to what degree asset prices— essentially, the liquidity of capital markets—would recover under the, presumably, revolutionary state of the world* in which asset ownership and/or the flows of revenue and collateral were reallocated."[9] (my emphasis)

Meister's core political concern articulates around how to insure the conditions of political effectuation of historical justice *in the now*, even in times in which the option of revolution-

---

9 Ibid., 230.
10 "I'm saying that historical justice can have value even when the option of revolutionary illiquidity can't be exercised, and that its value can be measured by the premium that could be charged for government-provided liquidity in capital markets—the 'liquidity put.'" https://www.salon.com/2018/07/08/scholar-robert-meister-on-a-new-model-using-the-financial-markets-to-fuel-historical-justice/.
11 "Options are versatile financial products. These contracts involve a buyer and seller, where the buyer pays a premium for the rights granted by the contract. Call options allow the holder to buy the asset at a stated price within a specific time frame. Put options, on the other hand, allow the holder to sell the asset at a stated price within a specific time frame. Each call option has a bullish buyer and a bearish seller while put options have a bearish buyer and a bullish seller." https://www.investopedia.com/terms/o/option.asphttps://www.investopedia.com/terms/o/option.asp.
12 https://www.jacobinmag.com/2021/05/welfare-state-class-struggle-confrontation-compromise-labor-union-movement.
13 From private conversation.

ary illiquidity can't or should strategically not be exercised.[10] This is why he suggests making use of the tools and language of finance, and especially the option pricing theory framework, *to characterize revolutionary justice as a financial option.* An option is, roughly put, a way of attaching a present value to something that is unknown in the future. In financial markets, options consist of derivative products that give buyers the right, *but not the obligation*, to buy or sell an underlying asset at an agreed-upon price and date.[11] As explained earlier, there is a price that is attached to the creation of financial options themselves—a premium.

Following this logic, and in elegant speculative symmetry with his understanding of finance as a technology to manufacture liquidity, Meister therefore presents democracy as a *technology to manufacture alternatives to revolution*. We know that, historically, the Welfare State emerged as an institutionalized class compromise following decades of hard-fought struggles, leading to what came to be known as a "social pact."[12] It goes without saying that the social progress resulting from this fairly long-lasting arrangement between labor and capital depended on a strong labor movement. And it's also quite obvious that after 40+ years of neoliberal offensive and ruthless financialization of our economies and social relations, the balance of power has shifted dramatically. Social struggles are crucially in need of updated political strategies. In the last instance, Meister's goal is nothing less than to offer "a discursive framework and political practice for the justice-seeking subject in the age of financialization, in the way that Marx did for the justice-seeking subject during the industrialization of manufacture."[13]

Concretely speaking, If the Welfare State was the political price exacted for *not* exercising the option of a General Strike, argues Meister, there should also be a political price for *not* exercising the option to bring on a liquidity crisis, let's say, through the means of a collective action aimed to occupy (i.e.

re-possess) collateral that the financial system is laying claims on. In other words: "Critically appropriating the language of financialization thus allows us to see more clearly how democracy can reintroduce the political risk that government will not restore liquidity to capital markets when they need it most."[14]

But what are our options exactly? What does it mean for a justice-seeking subject in the age of finance to occupy *this* time and space, to collectively incorporate the strike price of justice, knowing how notoriously difficult it is to challenge the dominion of financial abstractions governing our lives at a distance? Or again: if we are to bracket, for the time being, the actual recourse to direct action generating illiquidity events, then *what kind of otherwise liquidity-making practices can we imagine that wouldn't end up reinforcing the prevailing power relations?*

Meister's interpretation of option pricing theory generates a pedagogy of (il)liquidity that plunges its theoretical roots in a reading of Walter Benjamin's *Thesis on the Concept of History*. It aims at reanimating the revolutionary urgency at the core of Benjamin's political project with a surprising yet highly rigorous financial twist that emphasizes the now-time of justice:

> A proper description of our task is to understand why historical injustice is rarely redeemed, and yet must remain redeemable, and then to describe, as Benjamin tried to do, the exceptional (miraculous) status of a "now-time" in which another time is also made present and thus redeemed. This intertemporality of justice is not merely a matter of occluding the history's apparent losers but of the proper valuation of the present claims that can be made through them—and of *seizing a moment when that value is finite and calculable*."[15] (my emphasis)

This way of dramatizing *the financial time that remains* is highly speculative. All the more so when it comes to the question of *intertemporality of justice*, a key component of Meister's thesis that I won't be able to fully address in the context of this article, even though it directly concerns the very existence of the many worlds in their financial plurality.[16] What I find most stimulating in Meister's theological-political insistance on the finite and calculable is that instead of cloaking itself into the moral mantle of political infinitism, the idea of justice as an option fully assumes the core enabling constraint of finance, namely, the fact that finance is, effectively and etymologically, about how we deal with "endings," about how we make ends meet.[17]

---

14 Robert Meister, *Justice Is an Option: A Democratic Theory of Finance for the 21*st *Century*, 11.

15 Robert Meister, *After Evil. A politics of Human Rights* (New York: Columbia University Press, 2012), 248. "The real challenge is to develop a financial model that explains how the constructive value of unjust enrichment fluctuates over time as the political, social, and economic relations of the affected groups also change. This poses Benjamin's question of when to seize the present moment to redeem the past. Here, however, *redemption would, arguably, take the financial form of a preference on the part of both victims and beneficiaries for liquidity rather than running debt.*" (p. 247) (my emphasis)

16 "Optionality of the kind that finance illustrates is more broadly about synchronizing heterogeneous temporalities, indexing heterogeneous cultural discourses, tokenizing the relative rates of change within and among heterogenous systems of valuing and ranking—the list could go on. Such forms of heterogeneity no longer need to be reduced to a General Equivalent if liquidity can be added through options that can index their changes to those in other, disparate, value realms." Robert Meister, *Justice Is an Option. A Democratic Theory of Finance for the 21*st *century* (Chicago: University of Chicago Press, 2021), 30. When articulating this idea, Meister references this article from Economic Space Agency, "On Intensive Self-Issuance: Economic Space Agency and the Space Platform," in *Moneylab Reader #2: Overcoming the Hype*, ed. Inte Gloerich, Geert Lovink, and Patricia de Vries (Amsterdam: Institute of Network Cultures, 2018), 232–42. http://networkcultures.org/wp-content/uploads/2018/01/21-ecsa.pdf.

17 Peter Sloterdijk provocatively describes political infinitism as follows: "Political infinitism, which is the political definition of the left, has so far had to distance itself from all the rhetoric and practice of concrete community, because it requires a politics of the finite. Alain Badiou has recently reformulated the axiom of a post-Marxist politics of emancipation: 'the situations of politics are infinite.' False but clear: by reading it, one understands well that the metaphysical left proposes the infinite as a critique of the finite—which reveals the religious roots of any left politics of the possible and the real. (…) On the other hand, the piquancy of recent communitarianism is to clarify the conditions of a left politics of the finite." *Sphères II: Globes. Macrosphérologie*, trans. Erik Bordeleau (Paris: Librairie Arthème Fayard, 2010), 362.

Finance is indeed a system that constantly presupposes its own catastrophic end, and benefits from how long it can be delayed. To be sure, many worlds have come to an end before ours—just ask indigenous people all around the planet. Why is it so hard to fully acknowledge the constitutive limits of the world(s) we live in? Finance is traditionally understood as the transformation of radical uncertainty into manageable risk. But as it prospects for ways of generating surplus-value, the virtual body of capital generates highly qualified relations to futurity that challenges the very limits of our cultures of knowing and forecasting. This speculative movement calls for new ecologies of practices and knowledges to account for our current economic abstractions. How can we leverage our own capacities to take risks and enter into metastable collective compositions beyond what is deemed possible—or insurable?

The passage from a logic of risk management to worlding practices of shared metastability is, I would argue, a core component to reclaim and, eventually, decolonize finance as we know it. Liquidity irresistibly flows toward the one world of Capital. Or rather, it is its most concrete, yet inherently abstract, manifestation. Inversely, we need to imagine a *cosmo-financial pluralism* that doesn't simply take for granted the alleged superiority of the "commons" as a generic ethical, political and organizational horizon, but engages in inventing transversal manners of accounting otherwise that do not shy away from addressing the difficult question of the *(in)commensurability of value claims* through and between the many worlds.

Cosmopolitics of the kind developed by thinkers like Isabelle Stengers, Bruno Latour or Felix Guattari is concerned with more-than-human communities and the way they attune with their associated milieus. The cosmo-financial pro-

---

18 For more on this question, see Erik Bordeleau, "After the Attention Economy: Notes Toward a Cosmo-Financial New Serenity," in *2038 – The New Serenity*, German Pavilion of the 17th International Architecture Exhibition, Venice Biennale (Munich: Sorry Press, 2021). https://www.sorry-press.com/2038-the-new-serenity.

posal extends this view by integrating the promises and challenges raised by cryptoeconomics and derivative finance's affordances for new collective incorporations of value. *The cosmo-financial art of belonging in becoming foregrounds value discovery processes that are not confined to the logic of the market.* For what we owe to one another is not something in particular: it is the very unknown that envelops our existences, the zones of opacity and indetermination delineated by our more or less felicitous encounters. The *cosmo-* in cosmo- politics/technics/finance refers to the unknown constituted by these multiple, divergent worlds and to the articulations of which they are capable of.[18] At this level of analysis, we start seeing better how any UBI system always also imply an ethico-aesthetical appeal to something like an IBU, that is, *Intensive Basic Units* made of wildly (or magically) interested dividuals actively curating stakes into one another (ad)ventures, facilitating in all fashions the haptic experience of feeling through others (IBU is always already an "I Be You").

Theoretically speaking, the perspective of the cosmo-financial relies on a concept of value that foregrounds *the active energy of discrete assemblages.* This focus on the collective incorporation or embodiment of value is decidedly future-oriented. It is speculative and pragmatist in scope, as it diagonally cuts through, if only for polemic purposes, the perennial debate around the dialectic of exchange VS use value (the inescapable trope of many a zombie marxist), foregrounding instead a different set of concerns around the financial art of asset formation and new types of equity-based relations. This emphasis on emergent worlding practices with a financial edge also tends to displace the emphasis put on the question of debt, a perspective largely hegemonic in critical academic and activist circles. As suggested by Meister and others, finance actually offers many others tools of analysis to challenge and reconfigure our subjection to capital. In this sense, if UBI is indeed a cosmogenetic technique as suggested in the UBI Manifesto redacted by the Institute for Radical Imagination, I believe we need to explore in what way the prefix *cosmo-* calls for worlding practices that could more openly assume the activating powers enclosed in the financial art of asset formation.

Long before Deleuze wrote about the question of belief in the world in cinema, he was already prefiguring a politics of choked passages and (un)timely contractions, conceiving of artful differences as introducing a "freedom for the end of *a* world."[19] In the same spirit, I would say: *other financial ends of the world are possible*. But in order to decolonize finance from within, and especially so in the context of the affluent West, we need to realistically—if only speculatively—start to flesh out the type of claims to abundance we imagine for ourselves and the generations to come. And we need to do so not only in the mode of an infinite demand for income redistribution addressed to the State, but in a way that integrates the resources of financial theory to inform otherwise worlding practices.

In guise of conclusion, I would like to rapidly indicate two prospective contributions—one fictional, one IRL—pointing in that direction. In his suggestively entitled *Another Now: dispatches from an alternative present* (Penguin Book, 2020), ex- Greek minister of finance Yannis Varoufakis presents a thought-provoking speculative financial fiction that significantly contributes to opening up the gate of radical imagination for otherwise financial worlding practices. Varoufakis's book reads as what a fellow sci-fi writer with financial inclinations, Kim Stanley Robinson, describes as *optopia*, that is, something like "the best scenario one can still believe in." Varoufakis's Other Now happens in a slightly bifurcated universe accessible from our current present through some special warpzone technology. It unfolds as a speculative thought experiment in which a series of pragmatic and visionary measures have been implemented to redress historical injustices. In the Other Now, for instance, tradable, corporate shares have been abolished, thus damming the whirlpool of financial speculation until its torrent is reduced to a tepid stream;"[20] yet, a variety of equity-based mechanisms and stakeholding relations proliferate, alongside a multitude of community currencies, suggesting a whole array of alternative liquidity-making practices. Indeed, one of the most interesting aspects of Varoufakis' book is how seriously (and practically) he engages in describing the inner functioning of this otherwise economy he sometimes describes as a *market without capitalism*.

The Other Now emerges out of a series of political interventions that have generated illiquidity events of massive scale. One of them articulates around what Occupy Wall Street has or could have been. The problem with Occupy Wall Street, writes Varoufakis from the perspective of the Other Now, is that occupying spaces to reclaim capitalism is futile, since "capitalism doesn't live in space but in the ebb and flow of financial transactions."[21] In the Other Now, this diagnosis translates into a movement of financial activists led by the *Crowdshorters*. By successfully convincing a critical mass of people to all default on their utility bills at the same time, they were "the first group to demonstrate the vulnerability of financialized capitalism and the power of a well targeted digital rebellion."[22] It is interesting to note that this fictitious yet highly plausible scenario corresponds almost

---

19 Gilles Deleuze, *Difference and Repetition*, trans. Paul Patton (New York: Columbia University Press, 1994), 293. For a full analysis of this passage which concludes *Difference and Repetition*, see my "A Redemptive Deleuze? Choked Passages or the Politics of Contraction," *Deleuze Studies Journal* 8, no. 4 (Edinburgh: Edinburgh University Press, 2014).
20 Yannis Varoufakis, *Another Now: dispatches from an alternative present* (London: Penguin Book, 2020), chap. 4, "How Capitalism Died."
21 Ibid.
22 Ibid.

integrally to what the great political economist Dick Bryan has presented on different occasions as a proposition for a *Household Union*. For Dick Bryan, just like for Robert Meister when he insists on financial theory's specific affordances for determining finite yet fluctuating values in time, it is essential that "we talk about what is happening to households in new ways. *It's not an income distribution issue; it's a risk distribution issue.* We usually don't have the language (at the level of households) to talk about that. Financiers do. So they are able to impose risk because they understand the process. We are bunnies in the headlights of risk transfer."[23]

Early on in the alter-financial novel, one of the protagonists asks his double in the parallel world a key question: how capital is formed and accumulated without a stock market? The Other Now is described by the alter ego as a regime of "democratized inequality" in which every citizen is provided at birth with a bank account called "Personal Capital" (or *PerCap*) that includes three strictly separated types of fund: Accumulation, Legacy and Dividend. Salary and bonuses related to work are credited in the Accumulation fund, roughly the same way as it is today. Legacy is more innovative: everyone at birth is credited with an amount of money that can only be invested for productive activity purposes. "Babies are still born naked but every one of them comes into the world with a bundle of capital provided by society. This means that when they come of age and are ready to enter an existing business, or start one alone or with others, every youngster has some capital to deploy."[24] The third fund, Dividend, is presented as an upgraded version

---

23 https://www.youtube.com/watch?v=bEj89w-mZNQ.
24 Yannis Varoufakis, *Another Now: dispatches from an alternative present*, chap. 4, "How Capitalism Died."
25 Ibid., chap. 3, "Corpo-Syndicalism."
26 Ibid., chap. 4, "How Capitalism Died."
27 This was actually the name of the Sphere' Cryptoeconomic Design Lab held on April 22–23rd 2021 (check the Sphere Timeline on the website for more details about the event). https://www.thesphere.as/.

of a universal basic income. Every month, each citizen receives a monthly payment that "liberates everyone from the fear of destitution," providing "people who do not care to engage in business activity with sufficient income to provide priceless contributions to society,"[25] something that the protagonist provocatively describes as "a right to laziness." Varoufakis insists in contrasting Dividend from more traditional UBI scenarios: "The key was that Dividend was not financed by taxation; it was, rather, a real dividend that people received as co-owners of the capital stock they were collectively producing—even if they did not do what we readily recognize as work."[26] *Another Now* is keen in suggesting how active stakeholding in re/productive activities can be envisaged as a viable alternative to the corporate world organized around shareholding structures that are by essence ecologically unsustainable and extractive, allowing the reader to imagine a series of mutually reinforcing circles of activating reciprocity. Or as we playfully like to say in *The Sphere*, a research-creation project exploring new ecologies of funding for the performing arts: *you can't be alone in a liquidity pool!*[27]

The possibility offered by blockchain technologies to participate in the design of new protocols for networked asset formation points towards ways of renewing our collective incorporations of shared lived abstractions, i.e. the way we come together without becoming one, generating derivative value along the way. This concrete utopia is alive and well in the world of web 3.0: a myriad of monetary self-issuances that could be modulated at will, following the affordances of a given ecosystem and in response to the inter-species web of entanglements in which they are embedded. For, to paraphrase Donna Haraway's provocative and staying-with-the-trouble insight: it matters what worlds world worlds; and *it matters what measures measure measures.*

Erik Bordeleau

Circles, the Berlin-based project for a trans-local UBI network, is a good example of such proliferation of new forms of plural organizing experimenting with money as a medium for collective incorporation.[28] Circles is an original initiative leading the way toward what they call a *Money commons, i.e.* a confederation of local community currencies aiming to operate a civilizational paradigm shift in how we resist monetary extractivism by keeping the value produced locally within the community. What is particularly interesting about *Circles* is that it doesn't presuppose what or *who* a community is from the outset. Rather, it constitutes itself as a collective power to redesign the economic relations we are embedded in—a form of curated yet inclusive network based on an expanding web of trust. Contrary to most UBI propositions, *Circles* doesn't address itself to the State as purveyor of income of last resort (although it still needs some massive support to bootstrap initial liquidity—in this case, the funding is provided by a generous sponsor coming from the blockchain world). Circles empowers its participants to design a pluriverse of claims on the already existing wealth in society, reintegrating it into circuits of mutually addressed promises. Inspired by the work of David Graeber among others, Circles exemplifies how, at the end of the speculative day, money is nothing else than an IOU, an "I Owe You," a document that acknowledges the existence of a debt. The value system generated by *Circles* reflects this state of fact in its design by allowing people to issue promises unconditionally, and decide in which sort of relationships they want to be involved in and how.

Can we imagine the scaling of such a world in which a myriad of quality-charged currencies meet with one another, each of them carrying the senses and flavors of the community issuing and backing them? These different self-issued tokens would be a bearer not only of monetized value, but also an index of local expressive forces. These new modes of measuring collective outputs would catalyze new calibrations between the realm of the quantitative and the realm of the qualitative, providing a unique answer to the proverbial interrogation about what money can and cannot buy.

Finance as an expressive medium commands a logic of implication. Self-issuance is about exposure to an outside, but it doesn't necessarily mean a full-fledged exposure to the full contingent outside of the market. The advent of blockchain and distributed ledger technologies is but one new chapter in a long and complex history of record keeping, archiving practices and institutionalized trust that goes back to the origin of writing itself. One thing is for sure: whatever techniques we use to keep ourselves accountable, something always exceeds. Anarchic shares will proliferate away from the grid. You can get a hold on it as long as you pass it on. We live beyond our means and our ends, we set them free so they take us with them and this fills us with a strange joy, for we owe each other the indeterminate.

---

28 https://handbook.joincircles.net/docs/users/.

Art for UBI (manifesto)

Universal and Unconditional Basic Income is the best measure for the arts and cultural sector. Art workers claim a basic income, not for themselves, but for everyone.

Do not call UBI any measures that do not equal a living wage: UBI has to be above the poverty threshold. To eliminate poverty, UBI must correspond to a region's minimum wage.

UBI frees up time, liberating us from the blackmail of precarious labor and from exploitative working conditions.

3

UBI is given unconditionally and without caveats, regardless of social status, job performance, or ability. It goes against the meritocratic falsehoods that cover for class privilege.

UBI is not a social safety net, nor is it welfare unemployment reform. It is the minimal recognition of the invisible labor that is essential to the reproduction of life, largely unacknowledged but essential, as society's growing need for care proves.

UBI states that waged labor is no longer the sole means for wealth redistribution. Time and time again, this model proves unsustainable. Wage is just another name for exploitation of workers, who always earn less than they give.

Trans-feminist and decolonizing perspectives teach us to say "NO" to all the invisible and extractive modes of exploitation, especially within the precarious working conditions created by the art market.

UBI affirms the right to intermittence, privacy and autonomy, the right to stay off-line and not to be available 24/7.

8

UBI rejects the pyramid scheme of grants and of the nonprofit industrial complex, redistributing wealth equally and without unnecessary bureaucratic burdens. Bureaucracy is the vampire of art workers' energies and time turning them into managers of themselves.

By demanding UBI, art workers do not defend a guild or a category and depreciate the role that class and privilege play in current perceptions of art. UBI is universal because it is for everyone and makes creative agency available to everyone.

Art's health is directly connected to a healthy social fabric. To claim for UBI, being grounded in the ethics of mutual care, is art workers' most powerful gesture of care towards society.

Because UBI disrupts the logic of overproduction, it frees us from the current modes of capital production that are exploiting the planet. UBI is a cosmogenetic technique and a means to achieve climate justice.

Where to find the money for the UBI? In and of itself UBI questions the actual tax systems in Europe and elsewhere. UBI empowers us to reimagine financial transactions, the extractivism of digital platforms, liquidity, and debt. No public service should be cut in order to finance UBI.

UBI inspires many art collectives and communities to test various tools for more equal redistribution of resources and wealth. From self-managed mutual aid systems based on collettivising incomes, to solutions temporarily freeing cognitive workers from public and private constraints. We aim to join them.

www.change.org/p/european-commission-art-for-ubi-manifesto

One Income, Many Worlds

Jardines Sabatini, Museo Reina Sofía, September 2021

Performance script | Within the framework of
On the precipice of time - The Zapatista forum

Introduction

Gabriella   Good evening and welcome to all of you. I am very happy to be sitting here with you tonight. How are you doing? Here I am, as a member of the Institute of Radical Imagination, an international group of visionary people: we are a group of artists, activists and researchers. What do we do? Basically we ask ourselves questions.

Indeed we are all living through challenging times, as if we were almost "On the precipice of time!"

During these months in Madrid we witnessed an historical moment: the Zapatista contingent traveling across Europe. We have been inspired by their idea of *A world where many worlds fit*: it is no utopia! In the Sixth Announcement they published before arriving they write: *"In front of the great capital, a common milpa. Faced with the destruction of the planet, a mountain sailing at dawn."*

Together with my colleagues, we want to invite you today to a collective exercise of imagination: what would the world be like, if everyone could have enough money to lead a decent life? Yes, everyone! If no one should struggle to work or live? Yes, nobody! Can you imagine it? We asked those questions to some of you who are here tonight among us: an amazing team of artists and experts in their own lives!

Tonight we want to hear their voices about work, money and basic needs.

The microphone is yours. Please.

Discussion about society and work – Each participant is presented in relation to work. Some claim work is not enough to define identity or life sustainability. What comes up is: generation gap, gap between Fordism and post-Fordism, gap between creative and material workers, work condition of retired workers, caregivers, students, etc. For the next generation and for migrants, work is synonymous with: precariousness, lack of "after work" time, lack of access to retirement, a struggle for survival.

Jose Antonio Good evening. Can you hear me? Allow me to introduce myself. I am Jose Antonio, born in La Mancha, Madrilenian by adoption. I'm an active worker, an EMT professional, bus driver at the Municipal Transport Company of Madrid. Driving is my passion. The truth is, I started driving when I was 18 years old, and before that time I was already driving under my father's supervision, and without having a driving license yet! But truth also is, driving a bus in Madrid is a very stressful job, very much so! At the same time I am really satisfied with my job, as I do it by vocation. Nonetheless, shifts often start very early. Getting up at 4 in the morning and started working it's tough, really tough!

I personally enjoy keeping the bus clean. When I go out in the morning, before driving, I like to clean the bus windows. Not all the windows of course! Just the windscreen and the rear-view mirrors, because when at night the bus goes to the wash, some little drops dry up and leave some shadows I don't like to see. I'm sorry! Maybe I got carried away, but my work is my passion!

Sebastian I'm Sebastian! Retired. A very long retirement. I had a work accident when I was very young, 27 years old at that time. My job was in high tech: appointed to the manufacture of printed circuits. If you don't know what it is, it is those metal parts inside all computers and televisions. In my life I have never lacked work: for me a job was always available. Then, because of the accident... Well, thank God at that time I had a good salary, with a good purchasing power. Then we passed from the peseta to the euro and the euro destroyed my purchasing power. Anyway, I lead a pretty good life. Thank God it was a work accident! It made my life much easier, when it comes down to leading a decent life!

Sarah God! Yes God! ... One day my youngest daughter asked me "Mom, who is God?" and I tried to explain and said: "There are many people who believe that God created the world." So she looks at me like this and says: "Who, God?!" "Yes!" I say, "God, why? Who do you think created the world?" She replied: "Well, the workers!" Of course, I thought! That makes sense: the world is created by the people who do things all the time!

I forgot to introduce myself! I am Sarah: woman, 42 years old, single mother, with two very young daughters. I am someone who likes writing a lot, that's why I studied jour-

Jardines Sabatini, Museo
Reina Sofía, September 2021

nalism. And I am also someone who's always struggling with time! Basically I've been working my entire life! Sometimes in better condition, but most of the time in very precarious condition. So often one isn't even able to make it! One can't make the ends meet!

Amalia   Work is fundamental in the life of a human being. First and foremost it provides you the motivation to get you out of bed, it gives you a purpose. So you are willing to work. Also because in the end you know you'll get your reward, which is your salary, to afford your costs. Nowadays everything costs! No matter where one lives, you need to be able to cover your bills, and even more so if you are single like me. Not having a partner I have to sort life on my own. For me it is essential to work otherwise I drown!

Ana   The big problem with work is that it's linked to a salary. This is the big problem with work, right? One works to earn money. Somehow it has been instilled in me to have the things that are important in life—like a house or a family—you need to have a good job! My name is Ana, a woman from the province who dreams the countryside, and living in Madrid. I have managed to work as a psychologist for an immigrant participation center. How I love my job! Yet . . .

In the end life puts you there, it goes without saying, work is assumed as normal in people's life. One lives on a set schedule, in a fixed house, with a certain routine... Who, me?! that up until a few years ago I was the most anti-routine person. And yet now I have my fixed payroll at the end of the month. On the other hand I have lost the magic I knew before, when I had less (because I had much less!).

Lucía   Hi! I'm just a girl. A girl who learns as she grows up.

Mar   Hello everyone, I'm Mar Núñez, 55 years old. Don't care about my age, it's posted everywhere already! We are in this assembly to discuss precariousness, right? Well I have never made a living as an artist or an activist. I have always had to earn my living through other jobs: actually I'm a graphic designer, that's how I make my living. In the last ten years my job sucked 80% of my energy. As a freelance professional in the so-called creative industries, I need to use all my skills to compete in a larger market from a position of great inequality. I use my social relationships, my creative energy, my time, my dreams. I need to waste all this energy just to be able to merely sustain my life! Yet I would also like to be able to support my passions: art and social participation. For example, at this very moment I should be working, I chose to be here instead. So my question for today is: are we finally able to find a way to stop working for pointless or useless things?

Fears – What are the intimate fears in a precarious job market? To become homeless, to remain jobless, to face high unfair competition, the increase of poverty and consumerism. Sharing the precariousness of our lives becomes a form of subjectivation.

Constanza   My name is Constanza, I am a domestic worker. I came to Spain about 14 years ago. I am graduated in social communication. I did some work as a radio journalist and more as a primary school teacher. I also belong to the feminist

Jardines Sabatini, Museo Reina Sofía, September 2021

movement, that's what I do in my spare time. At the time, I was told the only chance I had to come to Spain was to work as a maid, so I said yes, that I would do it. But this decision cost me a lot, it really did! Currently I work just to survive.

Amalia I am Amalia, from Ecuador. I have been living in Madrid for many years now. I am a mother and a grandmother. Friend of my friends, a partner, and a woman who fights together with Constanza to defend the rights of domestic care workers. In my country I was a dressmaker, I had my tailoring workshop. This is what I have been doing all my life until I emigrated. Here in Spain I did all kinds of jobs, even those jobs I could not imagine I would ever do, but they allowed me to support myself. My priority was to be a fashion designer, I liked to sew, and everything related with beauty and elegance. Now I work with dependents and people who need special care. Mainly they are elderly or for any reason disabled young people. I go home to them and have to help them shower, dress, comb. I accompany them to run errands, or to the doctor. I also have to clean their houses, take care of the medication they have to take. Usually I start at 8 in the morning and finish at around 4 in the afternoon.

Miguel Ángel When you are poor, you are poor. That's it! Hi everybody! My name Is Miguel. I am the son of a waiter and a cleaner. In the Vallecas neighborhood I'm known as the "street nurse." Vallecas is one of those neighborhoods that has more of everything! If it's about social exclusion? Vallecas has more of it! Unemployment or school dropout? In Vallecas there's more of it! I have been sitting here in silence for a while, just listening, because I am very touched by what all of you are saying. I'm glad to be here. What beautiful garden we are in! When I was a child—I am talking of the late 60s—the red priests arrived in Vallecas to work on poverty, on social exclusion, on inequality. Back then all these words didn't exist, simply you were poor, period! Then Franco passed away, I was 13 years old. We thought social engagement and charity could change our neighborhood. But in the 80s heroin and AIDS spread. I lost many of my comrades. Death is no longer something I fear. There is actually nothing that scares me anymore. That's just how it is, the bare reality!

Constanza   I recently watched the *Handmaid's Tale*. You should watch it, it's very good. I had already seen the movie a long time ago, of course. I don't agree with people saying it is about a dystopian future. There's nothing dystopian in it after all. To me it is just simply so real. It's not about the future. Basically many of the things that happen in the movie are happening right now: we just don't want to see it!

Andrei   My name is Andrei, 22 years old, from Romania. I am a music producer, that's what best defines me. But I also have a job in construction. I am just a worker of no importance there. My greatest fear is to find myself on the street, with no help, with not even a place or a room where to stay. I am afraid of finding myself completely alone and cut off from society.

Juan Manuel   I am Juan Manuel, Spanish, from Córdoba, Andalusia. I worked in the administrative staff of a media company. I love children. Those I am in contact with are my

Jardines Sabatini, Museo
Reina Sofía, September 2021

friend's children. My great concern is they keep on growing in this consumerist maelstrom, and that they are gradually losing touch with personal values. It is so negative. I'm so scared that I do not even dare thinking about it.

Elena My most irrational fear is that something bad could happen to my dearest ones, and it got worse with the pandemic.

Rhythmic list
Constanza I'm afraid of unemployment.
Mar I'm afraid to be over 50 years old.
Ana I'm afraid of losing my mobile.
Lucia I'm afraid of forgetting where I'm from.
Andrei I'm afraid of to become a homeless person.
Elena I'm afraid of this museum.
Sarah I'm afraid of being forced to smile.
Hella I'm afraid of competition.

Hella Hi, I'm Hella! That's how my parents named me, after a German photographer who lived in Uruguay. I am an audiovisual curator. I am here on a scholarship. I guess I grew up believing that I had to work hard to overcome adversities. I remember once, I had to pass an exam, for another scholarship, and it gave me tremendous anxiety since I felt that if I got it, someone else would do without it.

Juan Manuel   Young people today have a really hard time when they come out of university or stop studying and are about to start their work life. Opportunities for them out there are getting fewer and fewer. And the contracts they are offered are becoming more and more precarious. I do not like to be pessimistic, but this situation looks pretty difficult to me!

José Antonio   Compare my children's work life to mine? Impossible! My daughter started working before she turned 18. She got little jobs here and there. She worked at Ikea for a year. I remember at the time she was trying to apply for housing at Madrid Municipality. They asked her about her working life and she told me "Dad, I've only been paid for one hundred and thirty odd days!" So it became very clear to me the jobs she did were irregular, her jobs as a waitress paid social security contributions only a few of the many hours she had worked. I am convinced the young generations are not going to make it to social security or get a pension to help them survive. Unless they are able to pay for private pension funds, they are going to have it very difficult. And even more so now that the economic trend is to privatize all social services.

Ana   I am very grateful for all the time that I took living under great uncertainty, it helped me develop this ability to improvise. Because yes, I think that despite all the work I do, I will have to improvise! I mean: I am not going to have the security of having a home of my own. I am doing pretty well, I pay my social security and retirement contributions at a high rate. Yet the retirement age is getting higher and higher. To be very honest I doubt in my entire life I am going to be able to complete my years of contributions to be able to get retirement.

Jardines Sabatini, Museo
Reina Sofía, September 2021

Elena I think I am going to get a pension. But I have no idea what kind of pension it will be. I guess I am going to receive a pension lower than my parents' and with less purchasing power. The one thing I know is that I will get to retirement in worse conditions than those we have at present.

Job precariousness, money, house – What is the real problem to be solved? Where to start to stop life anxiety? A starting point would be to make sure that everyone has a house. Participants try to define what the fair amount of UBI would be. Mutualism and support networks come into play when one can't cope with the cost of living.

Elena What does it mean to have a dignified life? A life with no anxiety? with no fear? With no precariousness? If you think about it, it's simple: one's salary should at least be double the rent. One cannot spend more than 50% of the salary on the house rent. In Barcelona, for example, one should earn at least €1,500. Oops, yes, I should have introduced myself. In general people say their job. I find it so sad: I am Elena ... 32 years old ... cultural worker. That's it! Is that really enough?

Juan Manuel According to the government, the minimum wage is around €900 depending on the area you live in. In

Madrid, for example, this is too little to lead a "dignified life." It should be raised to €1,500. Because if I want a decent home, I must pay a mortgage, and live with debt up to my neck!

Hella €600s is what I have been living with in recent months. Less than that is almost impossible I believe. Some months I had to ask my family for some contribution. When I don't make it there is also my friends support network, people I have been meeting along the way. I'm not the only one

in this situation. At the master I'm attending we are generating forms of accompaniment. In other words, in the last two months I have not been paying for rent, I've been living thanks to accommodation offered by my friends. Some friends are very generous indeed! That's to say: today it's on me, another day it'll be on you. That's how the wheel works. Juggling with the articulation of all these elements I reach the minimum.

Elena Maybe I have a very romantic image of work, because I love it and also because I am fortunate enough that I can live working only on things that are of interest to me. I'm not overly concerned with my income. But I must confess I cheat: I don't pay rent. It is an responsability I don't have, as I live in a family's apartment. The trick to being happy is to avoid high responsi-

Jardines Sabatini, Museo Reina Sofía, September 2021

bilities: I have no responsibility towards my parents, I have no children, I have no mortgage, I have no car. This is the secret of my freedom.

Mutualism – All participants practice forms of mutualism to deal with the lack of liquidity and public services.

Mar   Let's put it like this: I have different levels of mutualisms. The first and most basic one is that I live together with my partner, since to live in the center of Madrid it is extremely expensive. Then I have a second level that's to say: as a designer I belong to a work organization called *Mercado Social de Madrid* (the Madrid Social Market). It's about an economic model aiming at being transformative in the sense that it promotes work and consumer spaces which are responsible, democratic, egalitarian, ecologically sustainable. For example during the pandemic we created a common wallet, available to those who had more difficulties with their activities to pay their quota, so that they were not forced to lose their space.

Andrei   Basically, with my friends each one on his own, we wouldn't have been able to do almost nothing. But we got together, we shared some things, thus we could achieve something. We were five each one playing his important role: I recorded and edited the video, my other friend did the base and equalized it, then another friend wrote the lyrics and sang, another one, who has a driving license, was driving and what he earned was put on the recording, compensating also his fuel expenses. That's how together one can do something that one could never have done alone, no joke.

Constanza I live in a tiny two-bedrooms apartment, I share with a woman. My landlady is from Morocco. We get along very well and talk a lot. Pandemic united us even more, since we had to share a very small space and that brought us closer. I belong to the feminist movement where we seek ways to unite and integrate the struggles. My greatest experience was when I said my first "no." I felt I could do it because I knew my comrades were there to support me. In my daily life I often go around, sometimes it's a park, or a square, I sit there with some other women, that's how we get together.

Lucía I find it harmful not recognizing care as work. It is one of the many ways to make invisible what many women do, often are racialized women. I strongly believe it should be recognized as work and paid as such. If this is not being done it is mainly intentional, to invisibilize this burden vulnerable minorities carry. That's the reason why these minorities most of the time are caretakers, it's precisely because they are denied access to other types of jobs.

Introduction to Universal and Unconditional Basic Income. Participants try to better understand what UBI is. Could it be a support for the owners? And public services? Will it fail like communism in Romania?

Elena I am a member of the *Institute of Radical Imagination*, too. During the past few months—years—of confinement we held several meetings online, for sure less polluting than

Jardines Sabatini, Museo Reina Sofía, September 2021

taking cheap flights. We are activists, artists, cultural operators from all over the world: Madrid, Milan, Barcelona, St. Petersburg, Venice, Warsaw, London, Brussels, Rome, Helsinki, San Francisco, Berlin, Athens, Naples... Economic crisis hit everywhere. Yet, the air was cooler!

We wrote a Manifesto reclaiming (as artists) a Universal and Unconditional Basic Income for everyone. We believe that the UBI could be the answer. It might be the one and only measure today capable to solve the precarious conditions in which we live: UBI is the answer to the lack of security, the exploitation of migrant people, the recognition of all the care work that we all do every day, the right to say "NO" to shit jobs and the possibility of working for another generative world.

Sarah All this sounds great. Mee too, I am a UBI activist. Yet think about it: we are all here, in a nice meeting, we all say smart things. But let me play the devil's advocate: we would just be losing almost our entire basic income, to pay our rent to the landlords! After all, it's like the feudalism of our times!: "I own land, I own houses, I own apartments. The usufruct of my real estate provides me all the money I need to live upon: here I am, the feudal lord!" I think the real question is: what use would it be, if we got our monthly €1,500 basic income, but then we had to pay it all out ... rent, health care, education, transport, leisure and culture?

Mar That's true. But there is one more thing to bear in mind when speaking of Universal Basic Income: UBI is not just a monetary concept. It does not only imply money. It is more of a global concept implying the topic of quality: public health service quality, availability of public housing for a decent rent and a decent minimum wage. For sure the needs of a family having several debts and responsibilities, taking care of eldelry people and children, is not the same as someone who does not have the same responsibilities. What UBI is about is a concept of life as something we experience in common. This is no longer a generation of individual rights, instead this is the generation of the commons: we no longer long for personal bank accounts. I don't want a society of isolated individuals, a society where the individual cares only about his or her own personal security. This is the time of those who feel part of the common and contribute to the common. In such a framework Universal Basic Income makes sense to me.

Andrei I can say something about Romania. At present we maintain a kind of pay from 0 to 18 years old. The State pays around the equivalent of €10 per month. I think it's a good idea, but in the end it doesn't work as it should. Many years ago, in Romania the personal situation was taken into account: you had no job, the next day you were working in a factory. If, for example, you were alone, you were assigned a flat with one bedroom, a bathroom and a living room. If you had had a family instead—a husband and wife with one child—then you were be assigned a three-bedrooms apartment with one bathroom and a living room. Nowadays, with the regime change the house assignment is no longer there.

*Jardines Sabatini, Museo
Reina Sofía, September 2021*

For this reason, in the poorest areas, people tend to have many children, to get more State money, because they have no other chance. I think aid alone doesn't work, because it leads to such situations.

Conversation on the Universal and Unconditional Basic Income (UBI) and imagination: What would the world be like if Universal and Unconditional Basic Income was to be implemented?

Hella What would the world be like with a Universal and Unconditional Basic Income? Well, first of all I guess my jaws would loosen up, I would stop clenching my teeth during the night. It is a tension connected to life safety anxiety. It would be wonderful if it disappeared, I mean, being able to breathe enjoying a certain lightness, thus allowing me to be really present in what I'm doing. I think I would first notice the change in my body and in my mind. It would allow me to finally dedicate myself to research and explore my personal path.

Constanza I think basic income would sit perfect for domestic workers. Think of all us housemaids, it would give us the opportunity to do many things we had to give up to work full time in homes, for fear of not making ends meet. Who knows, I might join a senior basketball team, since I love it. One should also consider that a basic income for all, would not imply we stop working or we stop producing. Receiving a basic income would allow us to produce different things, in a different way. It does not mean people lie on their backs,

doing nothing. It would allow us to look for, and generate an alternative. With less economic pressure, I believe one can be more creative.

Andrei If I knew more of economics, I might have a different opinion, but really money doesn't grow on trees. It's no video game, where one gets money every day.

Juan Manuel We are demanding our young ones a series of things they will not be able to accomplish. At the same time, we reinforce the idea that they should have the late fashion sneakers and top mobiles. We are distorting the essence of the person, for the only interest in creating the larger number of consumers. So inhuman! If UBI were to be implemented, who could ever be against it? For sure those who have the reins of the present: the economic power. The almighty Mr. Money! All this seems to me a mere utopia: it is highly unlikely that those who enjoy large fortunes could ever be in favor of sharing them with the rest of the world. Our society is too rooted in power.

Jardines Sabatini, Museo
Reina Sofía, September 2021

Hella   It's hard to imagine. We are too used to the world as it is, with its conditioning and its own reality.

Mar   So where does all this take us to? To the defense of autonomy in our environment, to define our spaces for social and political participation in our environment, as well as our spaces of care. What I mean is, to keep a balance between those spaces is a constant drain of energy, so one would not be able to invest them in his or her own personal career. This is good of course, well ... I can't say if we really have to ... but implementing basic income is exactly what could allow us to negotiate better desires!

Sarah   As a journalist I work in a cooperative. It's a special newspaper, where I managed to find a space of meaning, also within my work environment. Considering my work is not alienating, let's say it does not expropriate me of my decision power: it is my area of interest, it is a cooperative where we are all poor, but we are all equals. In the end, we charge all the same. My workplace is a bit, what I would want our society to be like.

Costanza   I think that UBI would make us be less afraid of migrant people, since it would give us the chance to get to know each other better, not to fear there would not be enough to survive for everybody, or that someone else could take my job, or that those who arrive could take away what's mine. It would provide us more stability, allowing us to open up to the other, to look at the other in a different way.

Mar   We did not come out of nothing, of course! That's to say especially those who lived during the '80s—already 40 years now!—when this cicle of wild neoliberalism started. Our life habits are shaped by this capitalistic way of understanding the world. For this reason it would not be enough to transform our access to a minimum life income, we also need to transform our idea of what a good life is, and this is a struggle that starts within each one of us. Is a good life the opportunity to buy a low cost flight ticket to go to Pernambuco? I don't even have an idea or where it is, but I am ready to fly across the Atlantic just for a weekend? Have you got an idea of what it implies? Who's working like a slave to allow my two-days luxury holiday fantasy? Yet those fantasies are so embedded in ourselves! That would be a great reason for a Universal Basic Income: in a few year's time it is actually going to be the only way to sustain life since there's no work for everyone. And at the same time we need to clean up our desires. We must recuperate our capacity to desire starting

*Jardines Sabatini, Museo
Reina Sofía, September 2021*

from within ourselves and not under the influence of what's imposed on us from the outside! To get back this capacity as soon as possible is just as important as claiming for a Universal Basic Income!

Sarah   I really like ... What's it called again? ... your ... *Institute of the Imagination*! I think there is a correlation between imagination and time. We are too busy trying to survive that in the end this lack of time results in a lack of political intent. One can't transform things without being able to stop for a while to imagine other possible ways of living. A couple of years ago before the pandemic, the global movement agenda started talking more and more of climate change, climate emergency, it seemed like it was the right time. But who has this time to think now? Do we have time to think about how we want to face all this? The capital! Those who own the capitals are the ones that have the time to think and to imagine and so ... there it comes: green capitalism! In other words how to imagine ways to continue accumulating in a different framework, for nothing transformative, just the same good old thing in disguise! That's why I believe UBI would allow us not to constantly be in a rush, it would free up time for us to imagine other possible worlds, and it would also give us freedom to choose how we do things not to be accomplice in this massive productivity that keeps producing on and on and on!

Mar   That would allow us to regain the pulse of our life and feel that somehow we are all connected. Those are the moments I experienced great happiness, those moments when you collectively share the same perception. Those moments when you suddenly realize that you have the capacity to intervene in the construction of a common world. I may sound very abstract but I can recall that moment when we managed to do something in common in the middle of a square ...

In a crescendo
Lucia   With no authorization.
Andrei   With no need for authorization.
Ana   And it doesn't necessarily have to be anything special.
Aalia   Just the simple feeling that somehow we are building something together.
Juan Manuel   In a common space.
Hella   And we are doing it with a certain degree of spontaneity.
Juan Antonio   That moment you perceive you recovered your capacity of agency.
Sebasatian   As if the world was—with a bit of lyricism—as if the world was anew.
Sarah   And you could do something with it!

Finale
Lucia   What do you wish for?
Sarah   ¡Time!
Ana   ¡Playfulness!
Andrei   ¡Music!
Amalia   ¡Dance!
Sebastian   ¡Friends!
Juan Antonio   ¡Family!

Jardines Sabatini, Museo Reina Sofía, September 2021

Constanza ¡Sitting together!
Juan Manuel ¡Children!
Hella ¡Breathe!
Lucia ¡Poetry!

The mic goes around to the audience, to keep listening to its desires

Fade out

One Income, Many Worlds

Jardines Sabatini, Museo
Reina Sofía, September 2021

Based on an idea by
Anna Rispoli, *Einkommen.
Die Bedingungslose Rede*
(*Income. The Unconditional Speech*),
Wiener Festwochen, 2021

Concept
Marco Baravalle, Elena Blesa, Emanuele
Braga, Sara Buraya Boned, Gabriella
Riccio, Anna Rispoli

Texts
Marco Baravalle, Elena Blesa, Emanuele
Braga, Gabriella Riccio, Anna Rispoli
and 14 citizens of Madrid and Barcelona

Direction
Gabriella Riccio

Research and Interviews
Gabriella Riccio with the collaboration
of Ana Campillos, Maite Gandulfo,
Maria Mallol, Celina Poloni

With the participation of
Miguel Ángel Álvarez Tornero, Andrei
Alexandru Mazga, Sara Babiker Moreno,
Elena Blesa Cabéz, Amalia Caballero,
José Antonio Campillos Martín-
Consuegra, Constanza Cisneros, Ana
Gutiérrez Borreguero, Sebastián Laina,
Mar Núñez, Lucía Núñez Ortega,
Gabriella Riccio, Juan Manuel
Rodriguez, Hella Spinelli

A production by
Institute of Radical Imagination,
Foundation for Arts Initiatives,
Museo Reina Sofía with the support of
Hablarenarte / Planta Alta

Appendix

Author's profiles

Marco Baravalle

Marco Baravalle is a researcher, curator and activist. He is a member of S.a.L.E Docks, a collective and an independent space for visual arts, activism, and experimental theater located in what had been an abandoned salt-storage facility in Dorsoduro, Venice, Italy. Founded in 2007, its programming includes activist-group meetings, formal exhibitions, and screenings. Baravalle is a research fellow at *INCOMMON. In praise of community. Shared creativity in arts and politics in Italy (1959–1979)*, a project hosted by IUAV, University of Venice. He teaches Phenomenology of Contemporary Art at the MA in Visual Arts and Curatorial Studies of NABA (Nuova Accademia di Belle Arti, Milan). Marco is a co-founding member of the *Institute of Radical Imagination*.
marcobaravalle.com

Emanuele Braga

Emanuele Braga is an artist, researcher and activist, operating on the relationship between art, economy, and new technologies. In the past years he co-founded and developed several projects as Balletto Civile dance company, MACAO, New Center for Art and Culture in Milano, a squat and autonomous art institution, Landscape Choreography cross-sectors, performative and research project, and KINlab, an art space in Milano. He has been a lecturer of *Big Data and digital Methods* in University of Milan (UniMi). He curated and contributed to several publications as (with Andrea Fumagalli) *La moneta del Comune, la sfida della istituzione finanziaria del comune;* (with Landscape Choreography and Cohabitation Strategies) *Abecedario dei gesti del Futuro;* (with Tulga Beyerle, Lukas Feireiss, Jerszy Seymour) *Life on Planet Orsimanirana, A non-gesamt Gesamtkunstwerk;* (by Andrea Fumagalli, Gianni Giovannelli and Cristina Morini) *La rivolta della cooperazione. Sperimentazioni sociali e autonomia possibile,* (by Alberto Cossu) *artWORK: Art, Labour and Activism,* (by Alan Smart and Alan Moore) *Making Room: Cultural Production in Occupied Spaces,* (by Tomas Saraceno and Aerocene community) *Aerocene, Movements for the Air*, etc. Emanuele is a co-founding member of the *Institute of Radical Imagination*.

Erik Bordeleau

Erik Bordeleau is a philosopher, fugitive planner, curator and cultural theorist. He works as a researcher at NOVA University in Lisbon and is also affiliated researcher at the Art, Business and Culture Center of Stockholm School of Economics. He has published several books and articles in different languages at the intersection of political philosophy, contemporary art, world cinema, blockchain cultures, finance and media theory. A German translation of his book on the commons, *Das Commons des Komunismus. Eine Kartographie*, was published last year at Büchner Verlag (2021). In collaboration with Saloranta & De Vylder, he is developing *The Sphere*, a web 3.0 research-creation project exploring new ecologies of funding for the performing arts. He collaborates actively to Weird Economies platform, where he coordinates the Cosmo-Financial Study Group. He lives between Lisbon and Berlin and enjoys, from time to time, the discreet charm of the precariat.

Gabriela Cabaña
Gabriela Cabaña is an anthropologist and PhD candidate at the London School of Economics and Political Science. Her research focuses on energy transitions in the context of ecological crisis, processes of planning, value struggles, and the morality of work. She is a founding member of Centro de Análisis Socioambiental (CASA) an organization based in Chile working on research and public incidence in social-environmental issues. From CASA, she has participated in the delivery of lectures and courses on degrowth from a Latin American perspective. She is also president of the Chilean Basic Income Network.

Ilenia Caleo
Ilenia Caleo is a performer, activist and researcher. Since 2000 she has been working as an actress and performer in the contemporary theater scene, collaborating with various companies and directors. She has given birth with Silvia Calderoni to nomadic research ateliers on the practices of the performer and to artistic projects in different formats. Graduate in Philosophy, she completed a PhD in Performance Studies and Political Philosophy at the La Sapienza University in Rome. Her focus is on corporeality, feminist epistemologies, experimentation in live arts, new institutions and forms of cultural work. She is a researcher at IUAV in Venice and coordinator of the Arts Module of the *Master course on Studies and Gender Policies* at Roma Tre University; she collaborates with *INCOMMON research group. In praise of community. Shared creativity in arts and politics, in Italy (1959–1979)*, ERC Starting Grant. She is activist of the *Teatro Valle Occupato* and in the movements of the commons and queer-feminists. Politically and artistically she grew up in the scene of underground counter-cultures and social centers.

Maddalena Fragnito
Maddalena Fragnito is an artist and activist. At present, she is Doctoral Student at Coventry University's Centre for Postdigital Cultures. She is co-author of *Rebelling with Care* (WeMake, 2019) and *Ecologie della cura: Prospettive transfemministe* (Orthotes, 2021). Co-founder of MACAO (2012), an autonomous cultural center in Milan, and *SopraSotto* (2013), a self-managed kindergarten by parents. She is part of the research groups *Pirate Care* (2019), *OBOT* (2020). In 2021, with the activation of the iteration *Raising Care* within the *School of Mutation*, she joined the *Institute of Radical Imagination*. *maddalenafragnito.com*

Julio Linares
Julio Linares is an economic anthropologist and activist born in the territories known today as Guatemala. He is currently based in Berlin, where he co-founded and co-organises *Circles UBI*, a basic income system for communities, leveraging direct democratic practices and p2p technologies in order to collectively organize a basic income without, within and beyond the nation-state. Since 2018, he has served as public outreach for the Basic Income Earth Network (BIEN), co-creating the *Latin American Basic Income Network* and *Taiwanese Basic Income Network*, among others. His present focus is on democratic municipalist approaches towards bringing basic income

into being with *BIRAL*, the *Basic Income Research and Action Lab*. He is currently working on his first book, tentatively titled *Decolonizing Money*.

Gabriella Riccio
Gabriella Riccio is an artist, activist and independent researcher. Since 2000 she has been active as choreographer, as well as cultural advisor. Since 2010 Gabriella is engaged in the movement for the commons, artworkers struggles and the Italian movement of self-governed cultural spaces, where as a resident member of L'Asilo – Ex Asilo Filangieri in Naples, she contributed to the *Declaration of urban civic and collective use*. She is regularly invited as keynote, public speaker and lecturer on practices of commoning and governance. She contributed to EU participatory policy development within the framework of EU *Citizen's Engagement and Deliberative Democracy Festival*, EU projects *Cultural and Creative Spaces and Cities*, *DISCE (Developing Inclusive* and *Sustainable Creative Economies)* for Creative Lenses. She contributed to several publications, i.e. *Home of Commons, online toolkit for participatory development* (2021); "*Per un approccio sistemico al patrimonio culturale: usi civici e beni comuni. Il caso dell'Ex Asilo Filangieri di Napoli*" in *Visioni al Futuro*, 2018; "La pratica dell'uso civico come scelta estetica etica e politica per il sensibile comune" in Stefano Rodotà, *I beni comuni. L'inaspettata rinascita degli usi collettivi*, 2016; *L'Asilo as a case study* for Creative Lenses, and "L'Asilo" in *Models to Manifestos*, 2019. Gabriella is a co-founding member of the *Institute for Radical Imagination*.
gabriellariccio.it

Anna Rispoli
Anna Rispoli works on the border between artistic creation and activism, to explore in a performative way the triangulation between man-city-identity and to test possible affective appropriations of the public territory. The forms vary according to the conceptual needs of each project. For 'Les marches de la Bourse' she summoned Belgian activists of the last fifty years to a demonstration for the right to protest in front of the Bourse. 'Your word in my mouth' and 'Close Encounters' are city conversations about love, normativity and eroticism as political factors. 'A certain value' invites us to reincarnate the positions of several European activists in a choreographed symposium. She conceived the concept of the performances around income presented in 2021 at Wiener Festwochen Festival with the title Income. The unconditional speech and in 2022 at the Reina Sofia Museum in Madrid with the title *One Income, Many Worlds* included in this book. Anna Rispoli is part of the Common Wallet, an informal network of solidarity economy that pursues a "polyamorous relationship with money."
annarispoli.be

Raising Care Assembly
Raising Care Assembly is a platform that brings together people who struggle to redistribute care within and beyond their collectives. Activated in 2020 by the *Institute of Radical Imagination* within the framework of the *School of Mutation*. Contributors to this collection in *Questioning UBI through the lens of care*:
Elena Blesa Cábez, Emanuele Braga, Sara Buraya Boned, Ana Campillos, Jesús

Carrillo, Maddalena Fragnito, Pablo García Bachiller, Elena Lasala Palomar, Theo Prodromidis and Gabriella Riccio.

Kuba Szreder
Kuba Szreder is a researcher, lecturer and independent curator, working as an associate professor at the department for art theory of the Academy of Fine Arts in Warsaw. He has co-curated many interdisciplinary projects hybridizing art with critical reflection and social experiments. He actively cooperates with artistic unions, consortia of post-artistic practitioners, clusters of art-researchers, art collectives and artistic institutions in Poland, the UK, and other European countries. In 2009 he initiated the Free/Slow University of Warsaw, and in 2018 he established the Center for Plausible Economies in London, a research cluster investigating artistic economies. His most recent book *The ABC of the projectariat. Living and working in a precarious art world,* was published by the Whitworth Museum and Manchester University Press in December 2021.

List of platforms, collectives and individual contributors to the Art for UBI (manifesto)

Platforms and Collectives

BIN
Basic Income Network a group of sociologists, economists, philosophers, jurists, researchers, free thinkers who for years have been studying, designing and promoting interventions aimed at supporting the introduction of a Basic Income for all in Italy.
bin-italia.org, Italy

Circles
Circles a blockchain based basic income made to promote local economies.
joincircles.net, Berlin, Germany

Commonfare
Commonfare is an idea of welfare based on the recognition of social cooperation. In a time in which precarity, insecurity and loneliness are experienced by an increasing amount of people, Commonfare wants to support the power of social relations and claim back the right to joy.
Commonfare.net, Italy

Common Wallet
Common Wallet is a group of people with different artistic backgrounds who have managed to build the Common Wallet, a community based practice in Brussels. They are socializing their personal income, basing the access to liquidity on mutual aid principles. The idea became a radical socio-economic movement. Common Wallet members don't live together, they have different jobs

and varying income. However, they get to connect to each other and finance artworks that they initiate.
Brussels, Belgium

La Murga Cooperative
La Murga Cooperative launched a manifesto *Gent que treballa en cultura, per una renda bàsica universal i incondicional* (available online in several languages).
Barcelona, Spain

Il Campo Innocente
Il Campo Innocente Italian network of performing artists and cultural workers, founded during the pandemic outbreak to defend art workers rights against violence, sexism, and job precarity, and to demand for UBI.
ilcampoinnocente.blogspot.com, Milan, Italy

Institute of Radical Imagination (IRI)
Institute of Radical Imagination is a group of curators, artists, activists, scholars with a shared interest in co-producing knowledge as artistic and political research-interventions aimed at implementing post-capitalist forms of life. During the pandemic it activated the *School of Mutation*, an open re-learning platform that activated, among the others, the platforms *Art for UBI (manifesto)* and *Raising Care*. In September 2021 in Madrid, within the framework of the event *On the precipice of time. Practices of Insurgent Imagination. The Zapatista Forum*, co-produced the performance *One Income, Many Worlds.*
instituteofradicalimagination.org

L'Asilo
L'Asilo – Ex Asilo Filangieri is the first formally recognised cultural common in Italy, an interdependent center for production of art and culture, governed by an open public assembly and practicing self-management of a public space in analogy with civic uses. L'Asilo elaborated on Art workers income demands on EU scale in the framework of *Commons as ecosystems for culture*.
exasilofilangieri.it, Naples, Italy

POE
Politics, Ontology, Ecology space of debate and research among scholars who share an interest in the problem area identified by the intersection of three terms: politics, ontologies, ecology.
www.poeweb.eu, Italy

MACAO
MACAO independent center for art, culture and research. Coordinated by an open assembly of artists and activists and based in a former slaughterhouse in Milan. MACAO implemented *Common Coin*, a social currency integrated with a basic income based on social cooperation, and hosted the hackmeeting *La moneta del Comune (The Currency of the Common)*.
macaomilano.org, Milan, Italy

Raising Care
Translocal activists platform on care activated during pandemic within the School of Muations, Institute of Radical Imagination.
instituteofradicalimagination.org,
Italy, Spain, Greece, Serbia

S.a.L.E. Docks
S.a.L.E. Docks independent space for arts and politics run by cultural workers, artists, and students aiming to reverse the processes that privatize the art com-

Art for UBI (manifesto)

mons, addressing the relationship between cultural capital and endemic precariousness, the neoliberal use of art as a device to capture critical imagination and thinking, and the link between are art, finance, real estate and gentrification.
saledocks.org, Venice, Italy

State of the Arts
State of the Arts open platform to reimagine the conditions that shape the art world today, working on art labor and organization.
state-of-the-arts.net, Brussels, Belgium

The Lab
The Lab art space seeks to support traditionally unrepresented artists and to transform alongside artistic practices in order to engage meaningfully with visionary communities whose economic and cultural realities have been ignored. The Lab is *W.A.G.E. Certified*, a program initiated and operated by working artists that publicly recognizes nonprofit arts organizations demonstrating a commitment to voluntarily paying artist fees that meet a minimum standard. The Lab proudly adopts the *We Have Voice* Code of Conduct for the Performing Arts.
thelab.org, San Francisco, USA

UBI Lab Network
A UBI Lab is a citizen led group seeking to explore and advocate for a Universal Basic Income. Groups are themed geographically or by lived experience. There are currently 35 UBI Labs across the world, with the majority located in the UK.
ubilabnetwork.org, United Kingdom

Individuals

Andy Abbot
Andy Abbot artist, musician and cultural activator. PhD at University of Leeds with "Art, self-organized cultural activity and the production of post-capitalist subjectivity." Co-founder of *UBI Labs Network*.

Marco Baravalle
Marco Baravalle activist and researcher, co-founder of the *Institute of Radical Imagination*, member of S.a.L.E. Docks. Contributor to the performance *One Income, Many Worlds*, Museum Reina Sofia, Madrid September 2021.

Dena Beard
Dena Beard artistic director at *The Lab*, San Francisco.

Emanuele Braga
Emanuele Braga activist and artist, co-founder of the *Institute of Radical Imagination* and member of MACAO, where he experimented and contributed to *Common Coin* and *Bank of the common*. He contributed to the performances *Income. The unconditional speech, Wiener Festwochen*, June 2021, and *One Income, Many Worlds*, Museum Reina Sofia, Madrid September 2021.

Ilenia Caleo
Ilenia Caleo performer and researcher in queer studies and feminist epistemologies at INCOMMON, University of Venice. Co-founder of *Il Campo Innocente*.

Anna Cerdà
Anna Cerdà i Callís assistant curator at MACBA and member of *La Murga Cooperative*.

Appendix

Marina Donatone
Marina Donatone dance and choreographer, co-founder of *Il Campo Innocente*.

Andrea Fumagalli
Andrea Fumagalli economist, professor at the University of Pavia, focuses on macroeconomic theory, heterodox monetary theories, the economics of innovation, income distribution and the mutations of contemporary capitalism. Co-founder of *Commonfare* and *BIN Italy*.

Wouter Hillart
Wouter Hillart co-founder of *State of the Arts*.

Julio Linares
Julio Linares researcher at *Circles*.

Christophe Meierhans
Christophe Meierhans, theater director and member of *Common Wallet*.

Gabriella Riccio
Gabriella Riccio artist-choreographer, activist and researcher, co-founder of the *Institute of Radical Imagination*, member of *L'Asilo – Ex Asilo Filangieri*, Naples. Within the *Cultural and Creative Spaces and Cities* EU policy project, L'Asilo advocated for policies on commoning and an income of care and creativity. Co-director and contributor in the performance *One Income, Many Worlds*, Museum Reina Sofia, Madrid September 2021.

Anna Rispoli
Anna Rispoli Italian artist based in Brussels, member of *Common Wallet*, concept director text of the performance *Income. The unconditional speech*, Wiener Festwochen June 2021 and *One Income, Many Worlds*, Museum Reina Sofia, Madrid September 2021.

Kuba Szreder
Kuba Szreder researcher, lecturer and independent curator, associate professor in art theory at the Academy of Fine Arts in Warsaw. In 2018, he established the *Center for Plausible Economies* in London, a research cluster investigating artistic economies.

Salvo Torre
Salvo Torre researcher in political ecology and co-founder of *Politics, Ontology, Ecology*.

All rights reserved.
No part of this publication may be reproduced,
stored in a retrieval system, or trasmitted
in any form or by any means without the prior
permission of the publisher. Any breach of
copyright and intellectual property laws shall
be persecuted in accordance with the law.